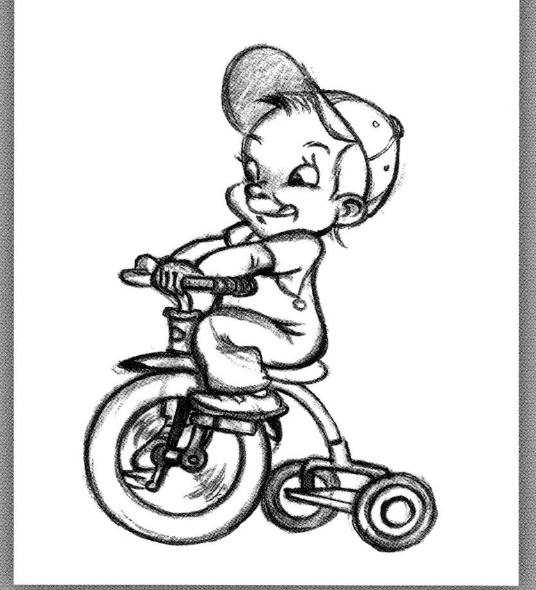

CARTOONING 1

Cartoons can charm. They can make you laugh. They can tell thrilling tales. And often, they do all three at the same time. What comes to mind when you think of cartooning? Comic strips and cartoons are only a few of the venues open to cartoonists. Cartoons also adorn and populate greeting cards, children's books, and advertisements. All you need to get started are a few books, some basic techniques, and a little imagination.

— *Jack Keely*

CONTENTS

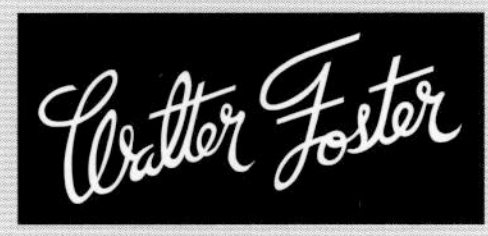

TOOLS & MATERIALS

You don't need many tools to get started. One famous cartoon character began his career as a doodle made with a felt-tip marker on a napkin. However, a few basic supplies will make life a lot easier for the budding cartoonist.

THE BASICS

For starters, you'll need a pencil for rough sketches, an eraser, some paper to draw on, and a pen or marker to ink in your final drawings. Here are a few general tips to steer you through the sea of supplies.

Dip Pen

An old-fashioned crow-quill pen with black india ink can make cartoons extra expressive. These funky-looking pens come with many different nibs—from very fine tips to broad-edged, chisel points. (Start off with a medium-point pen because it's the easiest one to use and the most versatile.)

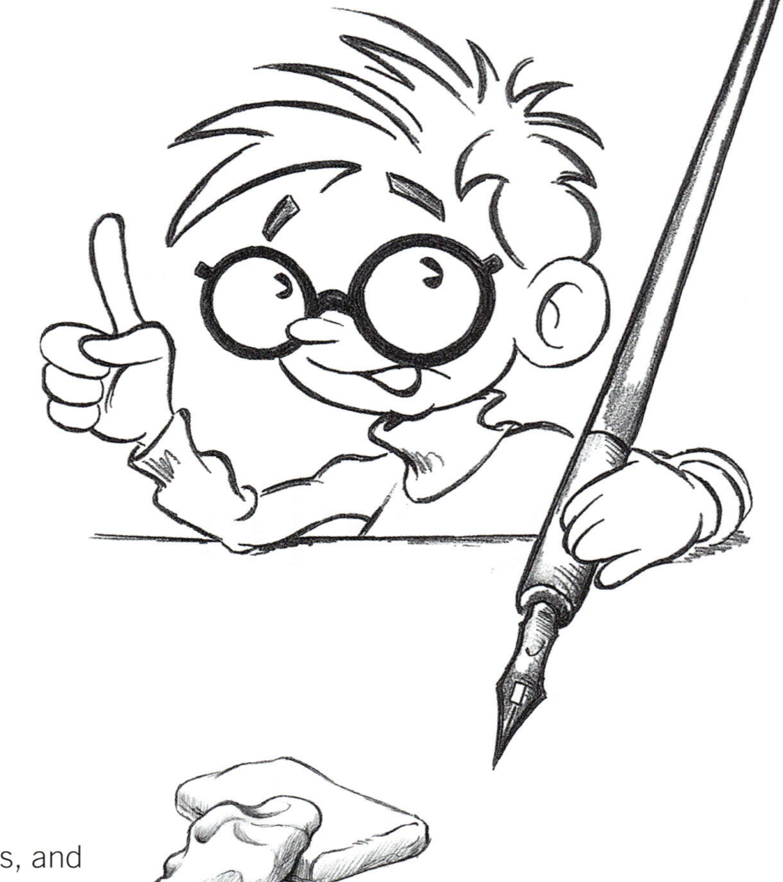

Drawing Pencil

Pencils have different degrees of hardness. H pencils have hard leads, and B pencils have soft ones. An HB is somewhere in the middle, with a lead that is hard enough to keep a point and soft enough to shade with, making it a good pencil for sketching. Use an HB pencil to sketch in guidelines and work out details on your cartoons.

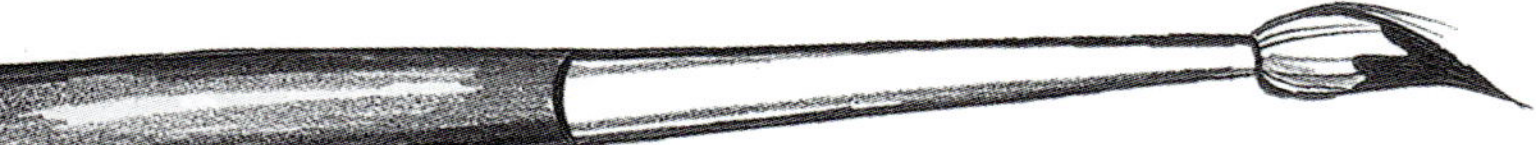

Eraser

A kneaded eraser doesn't leave crumbs, and you can shape it into a point to get into small areas.

Brush

The fluid lines of a brush and black ink can be delicate and precise or boldly dramatic, depending on the amount of pressure you use. A brush is also good for filling in large areas of black.

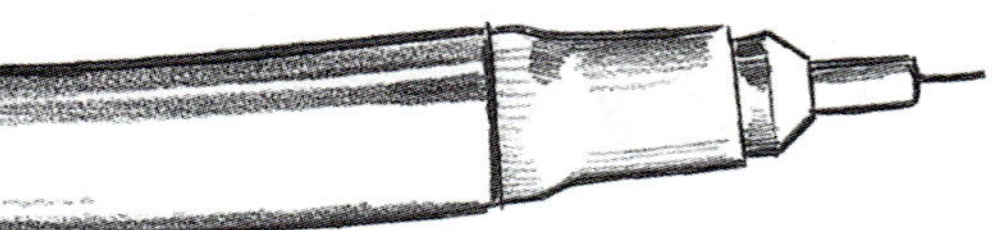

Technical Pen

These pens come in a wide variety of points, enabling you to vary your line widths. The lines created are consistently even and precise, and are fun to use if you do a lot of minute crosshatching or stippling.

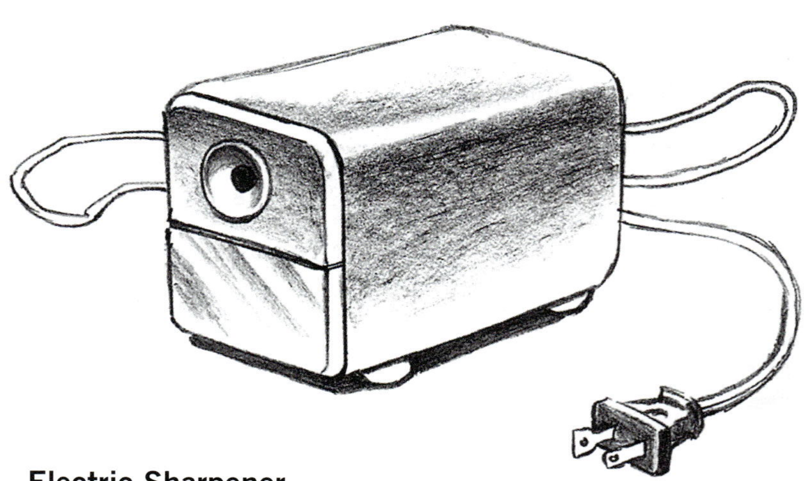

Electric Sharpener

Oh sure, it's a luxury, and you can sharpen pencils by hand, but an electric one gives you a great point and makes a satisfying noise.

Extra, Extra!

As you progress, you'll find your collection of art supplies growing. You'll want an adjustable lamp to shed some light on your subject. And you'll be cutting up a lot of paper, so a good pair of scissors or an artist's razor knife is essential. Don't forget a drafting brush to whisk away eraser crumbs and other debris from your masterpiece—and a T-square and a couple of triangles will be invaluable if you decide to start laying out your own comic strips. Finally, drafting tape will hold your drawing securely in place on your desk or drafting board.

Light It

Work out all the details in your cartoon on tracing paper, and then tape the sketch to a light box with drafting tape. Place a piece of smooth-finish, heavyweight paper over the sketch, turn on the light, and trace it in ink. *Voilà!*

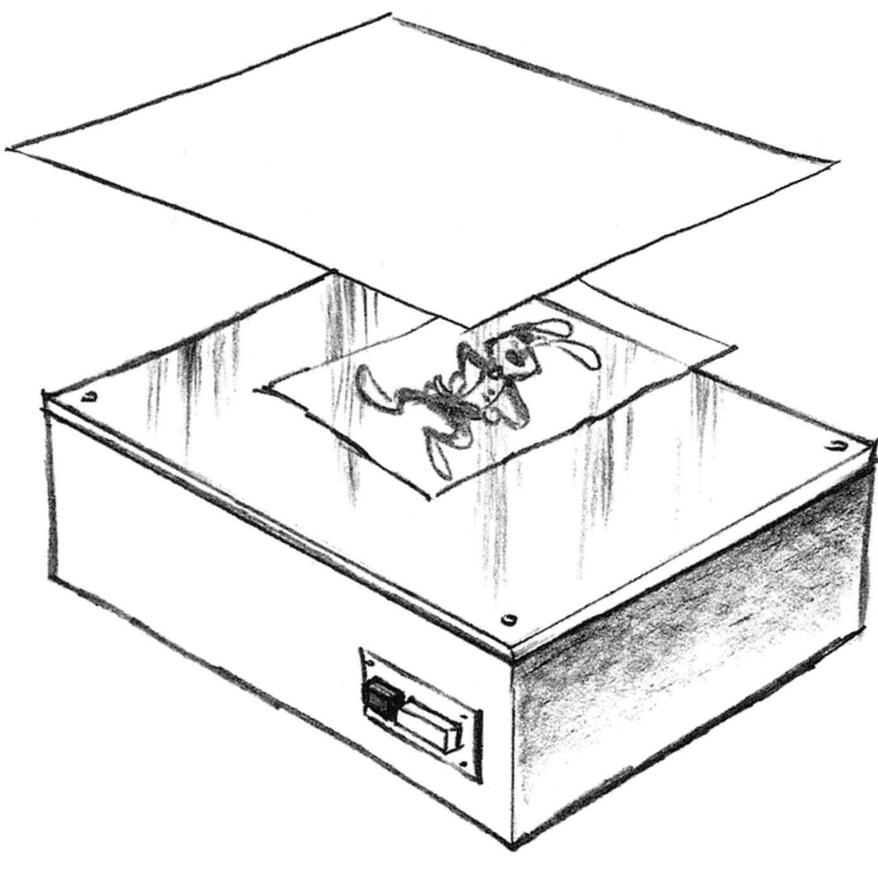

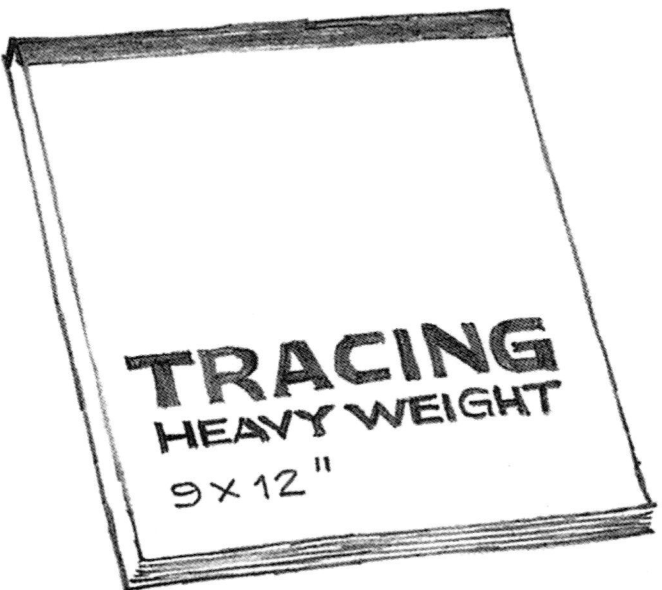

Paper Training

Play around with different types of paper and drawing surfaces. The texture of the surface will affect the kinds of lines you can produce. You'll need a smooth surface for precise, clean lines, but rough paper may suit you if you're after a textured, artsy effect.

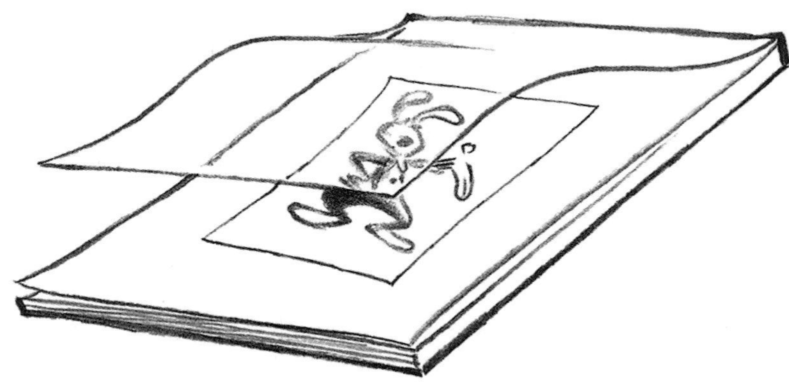

Trace It

If you prefer working on tracing paper but want your final cartoon to be on a thick paper stock, first ink over your masterpiece on tracing paper, and then photocopy it onto card stock.

WHICH WAY?

There's more than one route to Cartoon Town. Remember, this is an art, not a science, and you can make up a lot of your own rules. Don't be afraid to break out of the mold. Cartoons can be cute, cuddly, wacky, weird, thrilling, or chilling, depending on who's steering the pen. And in an arena where bugs wear clothes, mild-mannered reporters moonlight as superheroes, and teapots talk, anything goes.

In this book, you'll see three different approaches—three sets of guidelines for creating different types of cartoons. Try the different styles on for size and see which one fits you best.

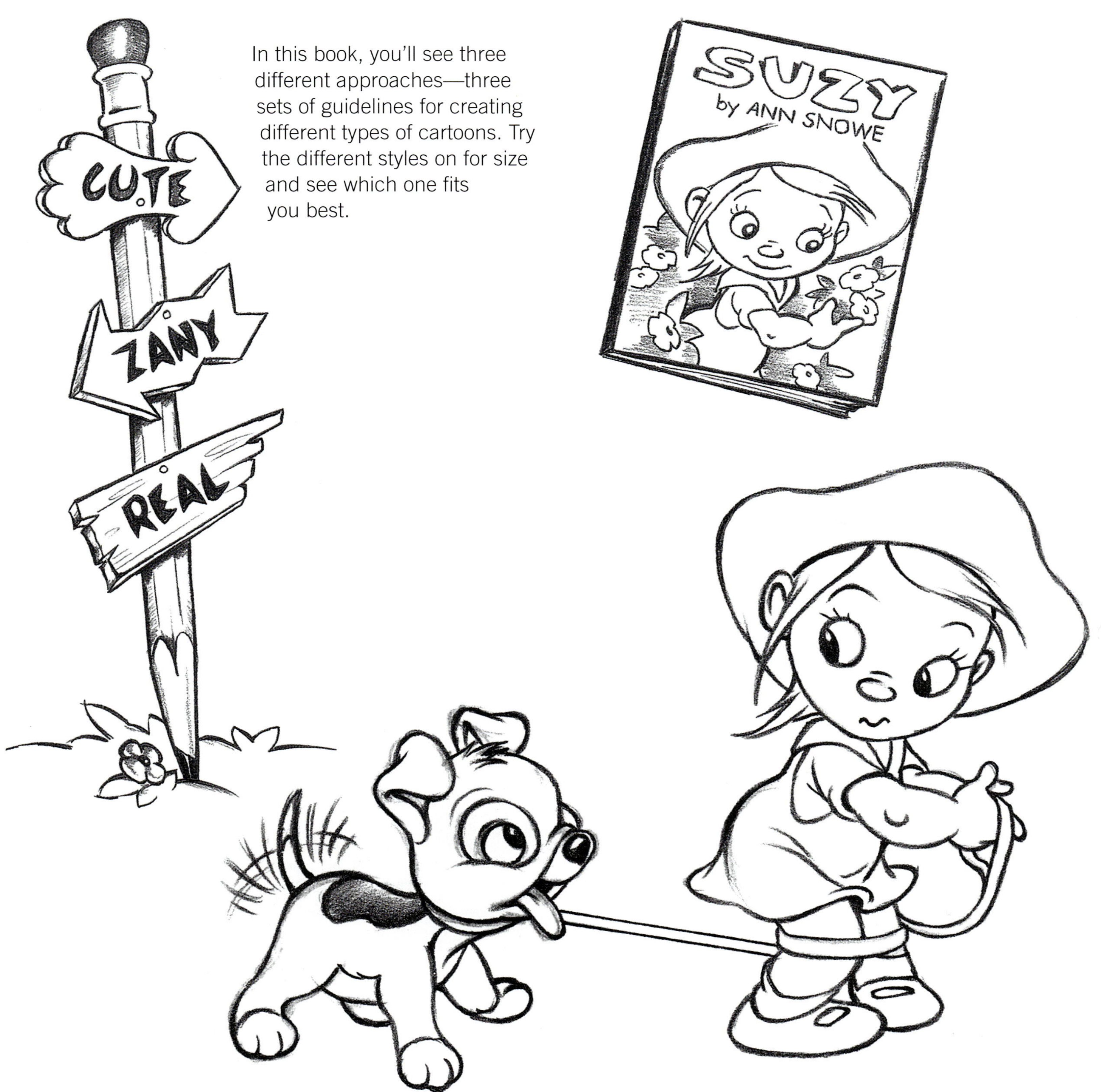

Cute Cartoons

A lot of comic strips, children's books, and greeting cards are populated by precocious, big-eyed moppets and their lovable furry friends. These characters are endlessly produced as collectible figurines and ornaments as well. There's nothing like a little kid or a puppy to bring out warm and fuzzy feelings in even the grumpiest reader.

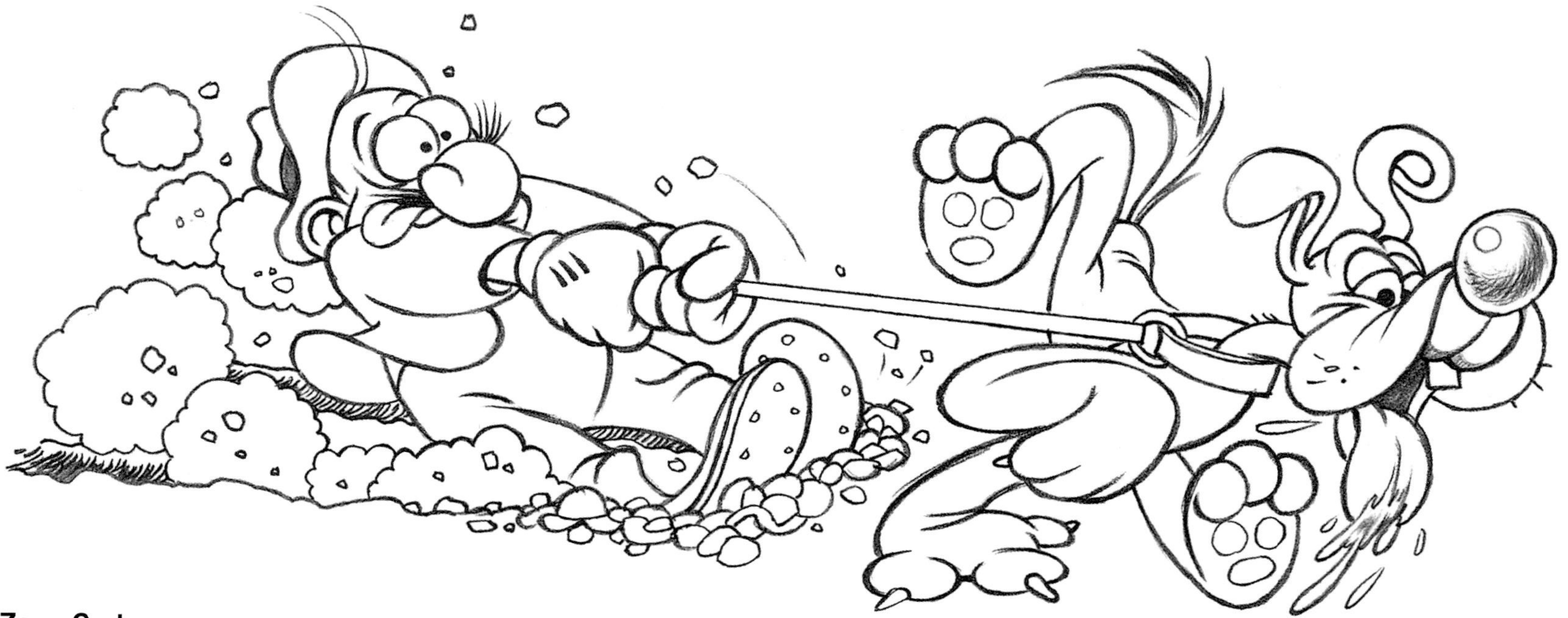

Zany Cartoons

The wild characters and slapstick humor of zany cartoons are a warped reflection of our world. The situations the characters find themselves in are often familiar to us (late for work, annoyed by a neighbor, or babysitting a brat, for instance), and their ridiculous responses are wildly exaggerated versions of our own.

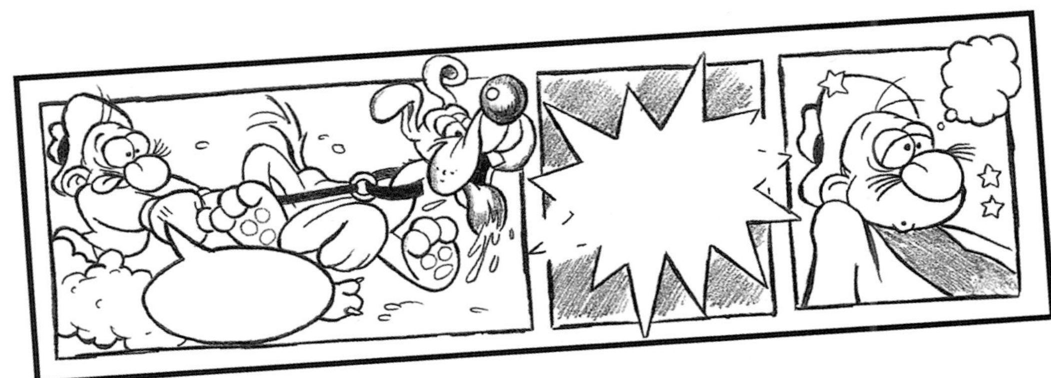

Realistic Cartoons

Cartoon realism isn't exactly realistic. Everything is stylized and stripped of extraneous details for maximum impact. Realistic cartoons display a knowledge of anatomy and perspective presented in a stylized version where everything is simplified.

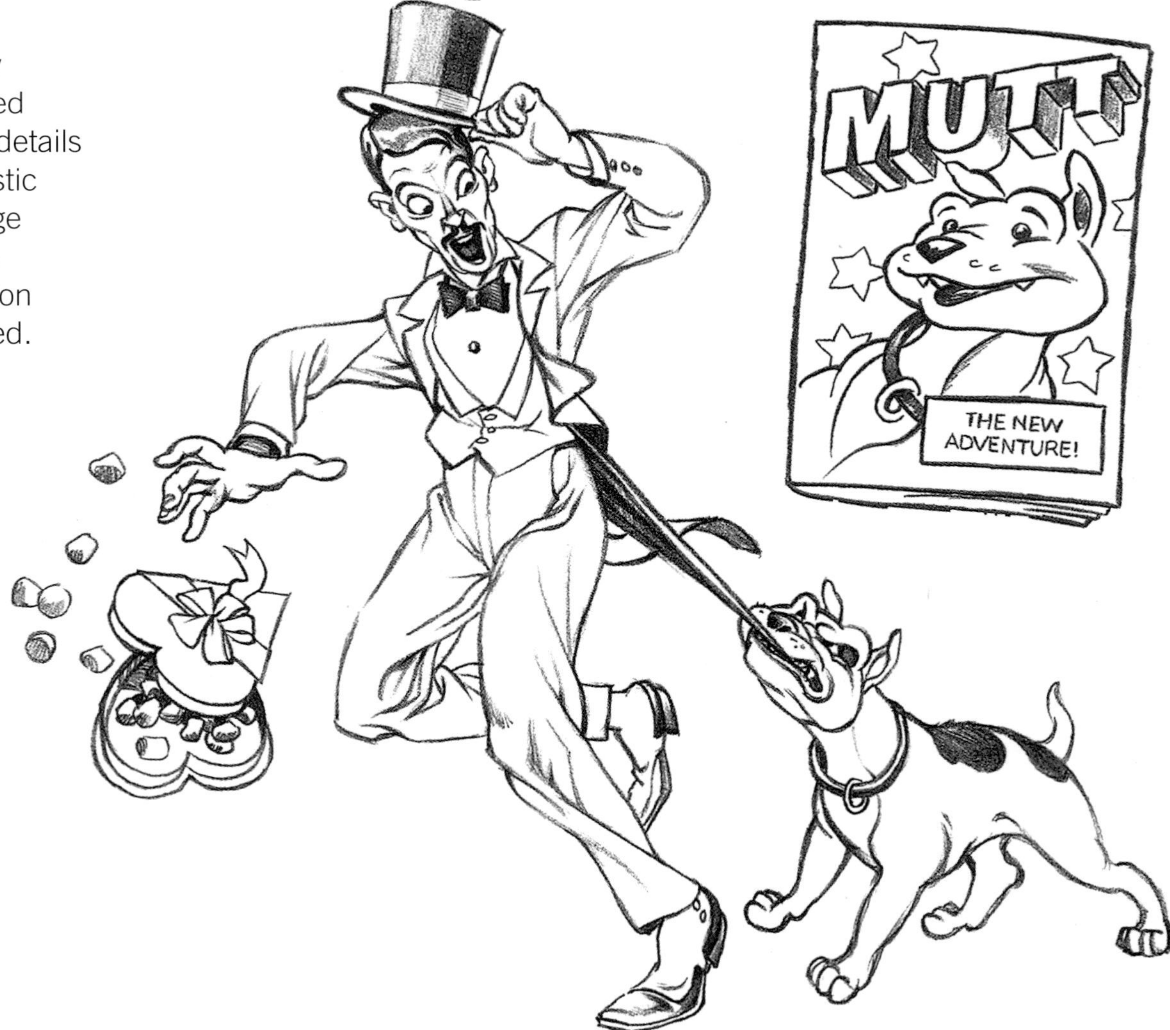

THE CUTE CREW

The cuties in these cartoons often have infant proportions—big heads; small, pear-shaped bodies; and chubby arms and legs. Tiny feet look cute on kids, and oversized paws make a kitten or puppy adorable. Look at the common characteristics in the cartoons on these pages, and notice how "round" they appear.

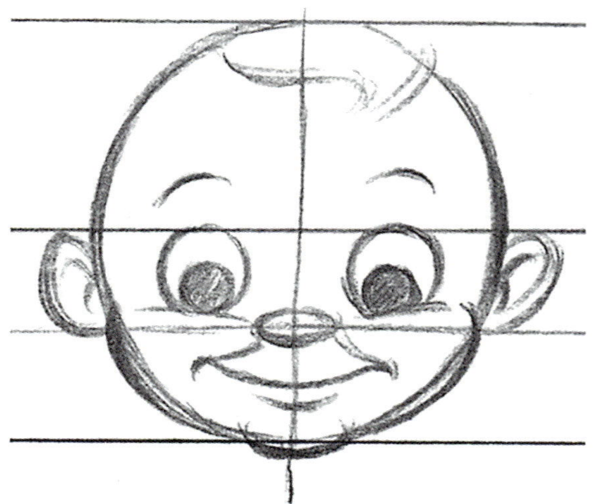

Baby Face
The basic formula for designing a cute expression is to locate the eyes, ears, nose, and mouth in the lower half of the face. Also, make the eyes large, round, and trusting, and space them wide apart.

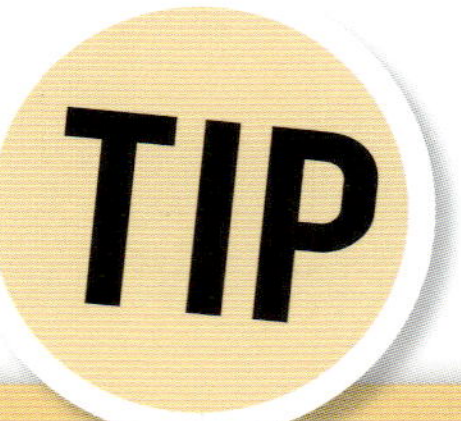

TIP

A graphic, stylized cartoon technique works well for advertising and trademarks, where you need a fast read and won't need to create a lot of varying emotions.

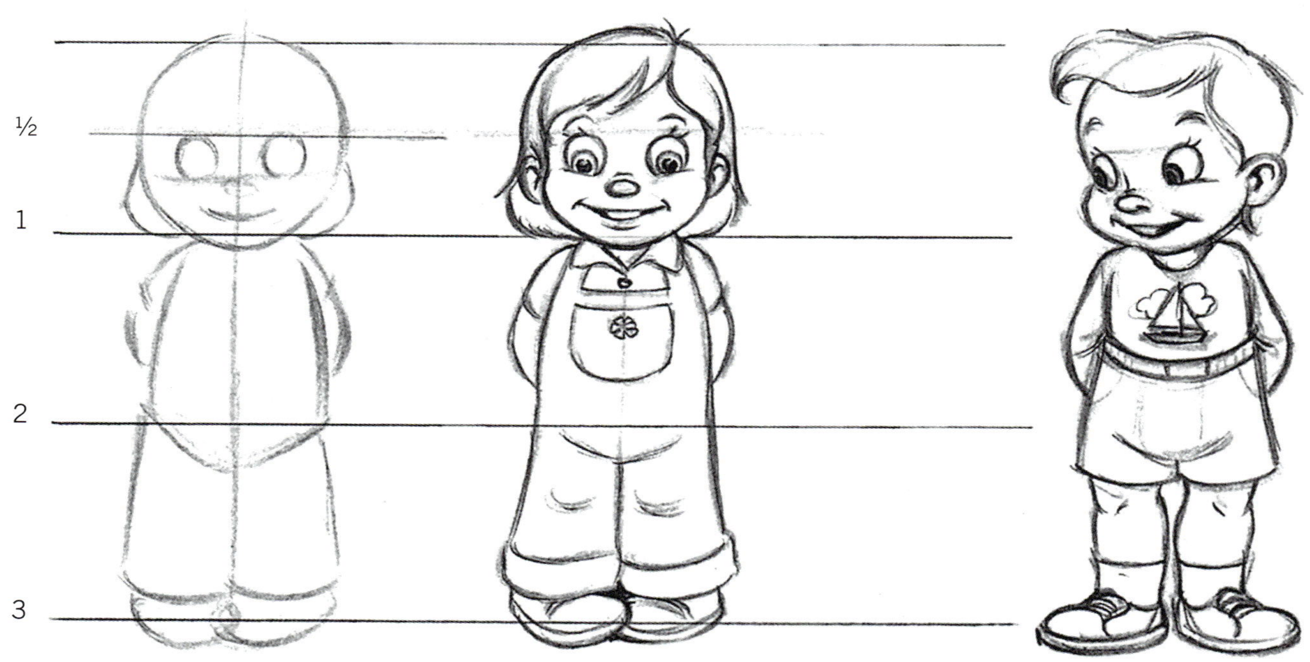

Size Counts
Cartoon characters are measured in heads. Cute characters' heads are very large in proportion to their bodies. The little tykes above were drawn three heads high.

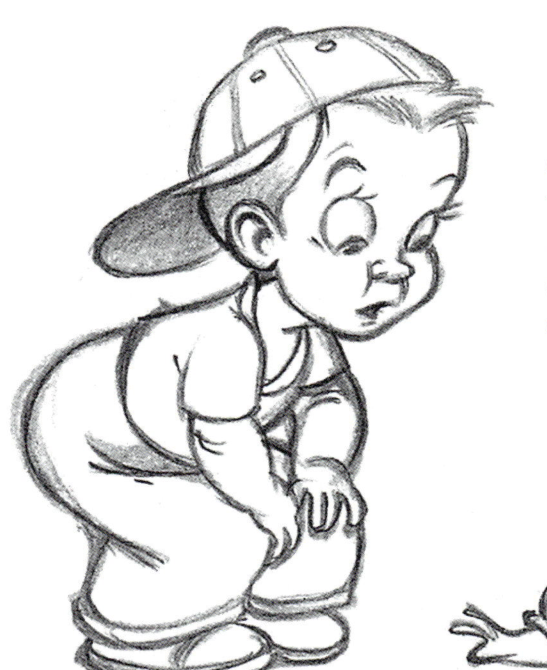

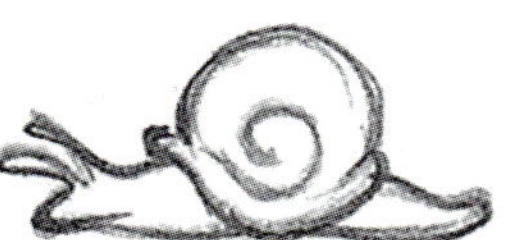

Curiouser & Curiouser
This little nature lover has his hands resting on his knees in a childlike manner as he bends over to greet a new friend.

Enchanting Extras
This is a pencil sketch that started out rough and was recopied with tracing paper several times until the artist arrived at the finished drawing. Notice how the tip of the tongue sticking out adds to the "cute" quotient.

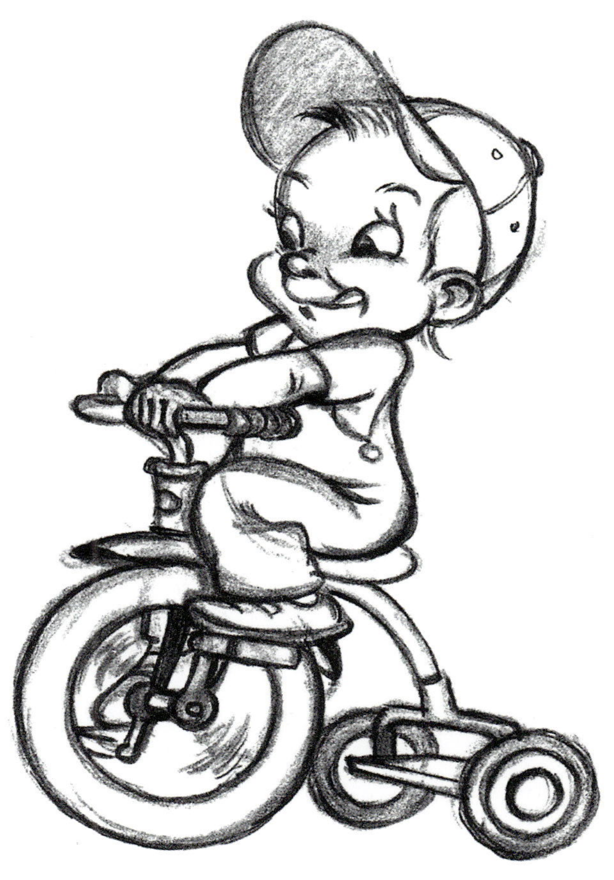

Bright Eyes

Little kids' eyes are large in relation to their faces. Cartoonists capitalize on this fact, and it's standard practice to draw innocent characters with big round peepers. Large, round eyes "read" well on the page because they are very expressive. You can create a variety of expressions by rotating the irises from side to side or raising and lowering the eyelid.

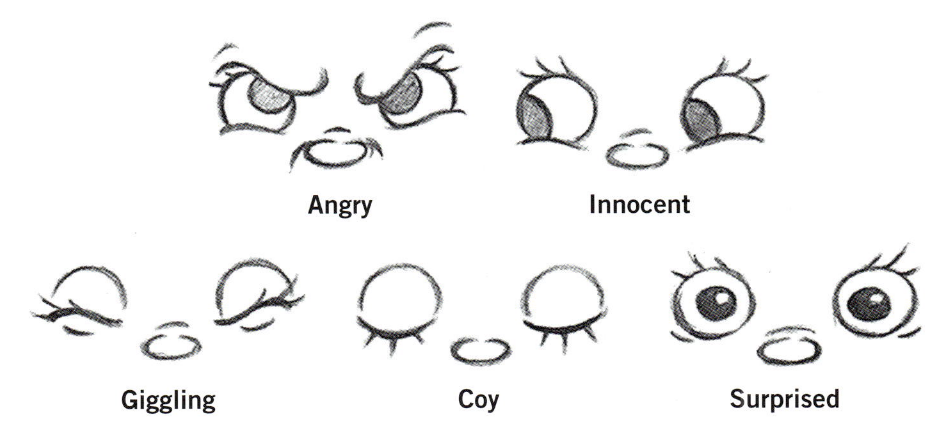

CUTE EXPRESSIONS

The faces of cuties can display a wide range of emotion. A few lines can quickly render a cranky pout, a look of wide-eyed wonder, or a happy grin. But don't overdo the details! Deeply furrowed brows and gnashing teeth are inappropriate here. It's simplicity that gives these babes their charm.

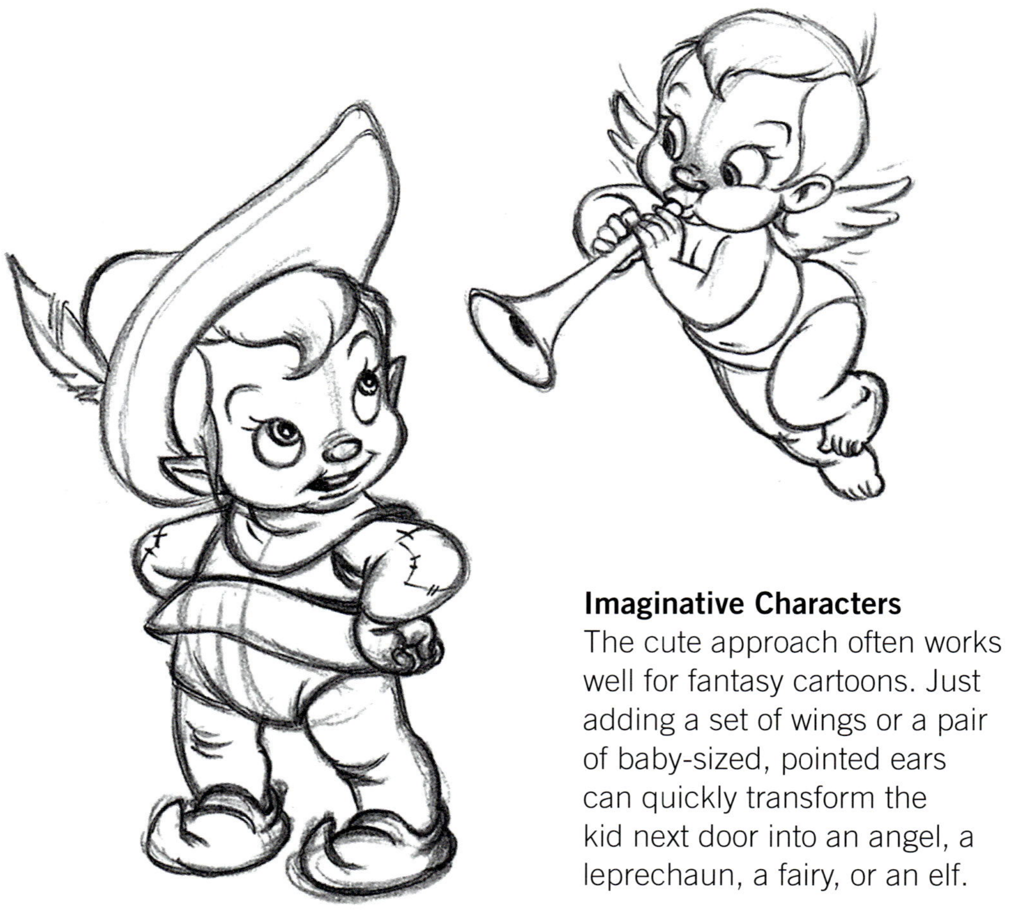

Imaginative Characters
The cute approach often works well for fantasy cartoons. Just adding a set of wings or a pair of baby-sized, pointed ears can quickly transform the kid next door into an angel, a leprechaun, a fairy, or an elf.

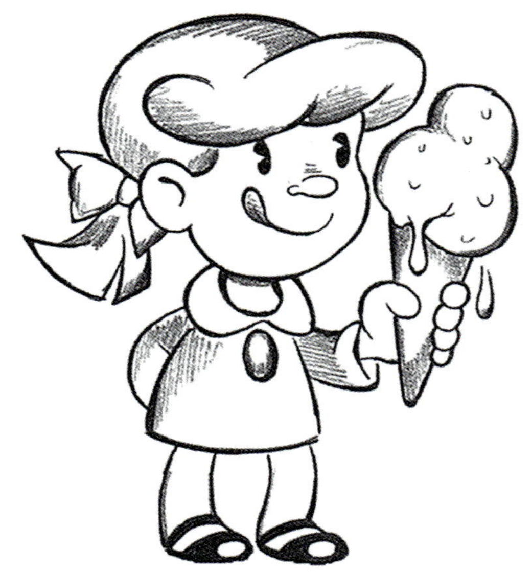

Simply Charming
This ice cream lover shows a more stylized method of drawing a cute character. She has also been drawn with more extreme proportions—the head is as big as the body, and giving her an oversized hand draws attention to the enormous ice-cream cone. Her facial features, hair, and clothing are simple and graphic, making her as cute as pie.

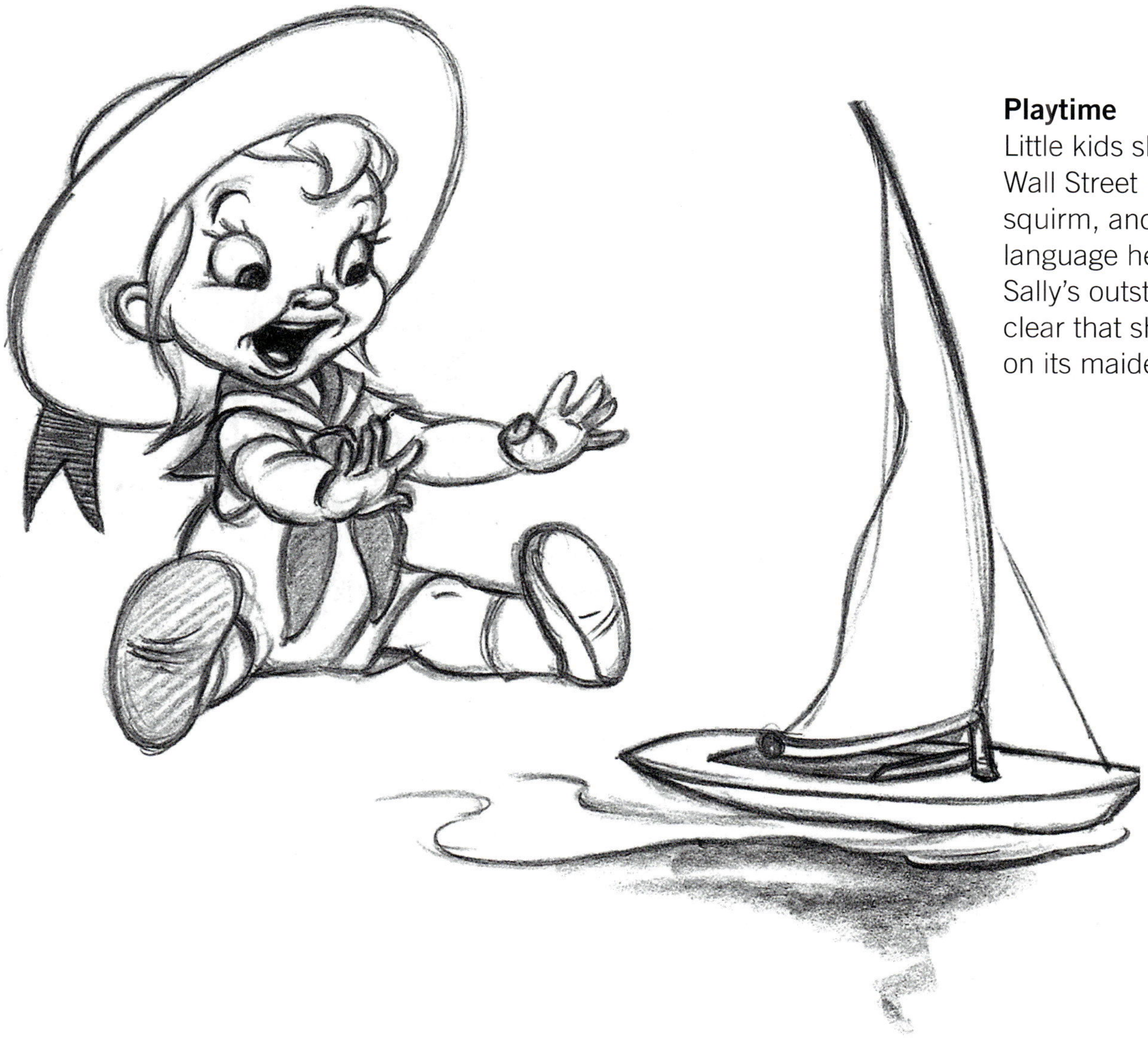

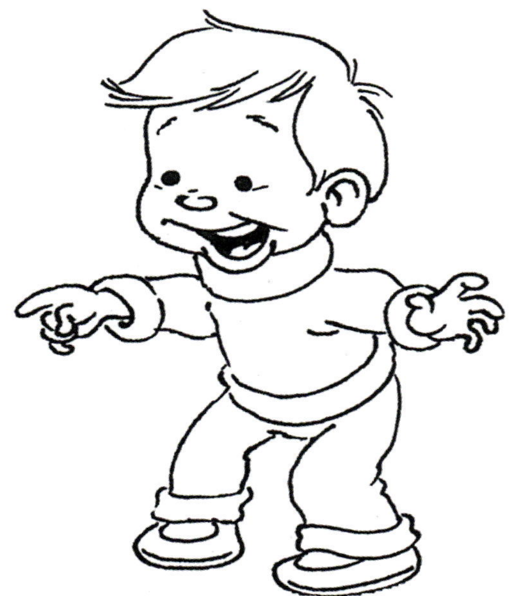

Playtime
Little kids shouldn't look as stiff as Wall Street bankers. Children twist, squirm, and jump. Expressive body language helps tell the story. Sailor Sally's outstretched hands make it clear that she's just sent her sailboat on its maiden voyage.

Who's Got the Button?
This curious cutie has small, button eyes, which can be very effective for creating a cute expression in a simple, graphic-style drawing like this.

Stretch and Squash
By stretching the face and making it taller, you can create a surprised or frightened look. Squashing the head down accentuates a pout or angry expression. This approach becomes even more exaggerated when drawing zany characters.

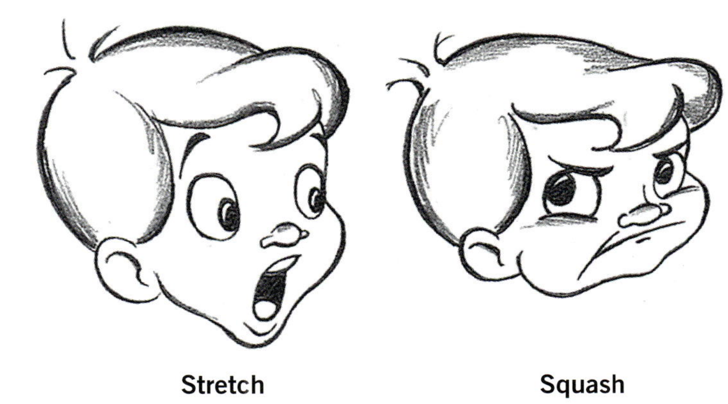

WARM & FUZZY

Cute cartoon animals are often slightly anthropomorphized, meaning they've been given certain human characteristics. Often the dark button eyes of animals are replaced with human-style eyes and eyelashes, and occasionally, eyebrows. In addition, their mouths are frequently curved into an appealing smile.

SMALL WONDERS

The basic cute construction is a combination of circles, ovals, and rounded "friendly" shapes. (Save sharp angles for a wicked witch!) Almost any animal you can think of can be cute when drawn with this design formula. The little animals on these pages are animated and lively, reflecting the actions of real baby animals. Making quick sketches from life of your own pets, zoo animals, or squirrels in the park will help you get a feeling for how animals move.

Putting It in Proportion
The design of the cute animal face is the same as the one for the cute kid face. Locate the eyes, nose, and mouth in the lower half. The eyes are large and round. Chubby cheeks overlap the eyes.

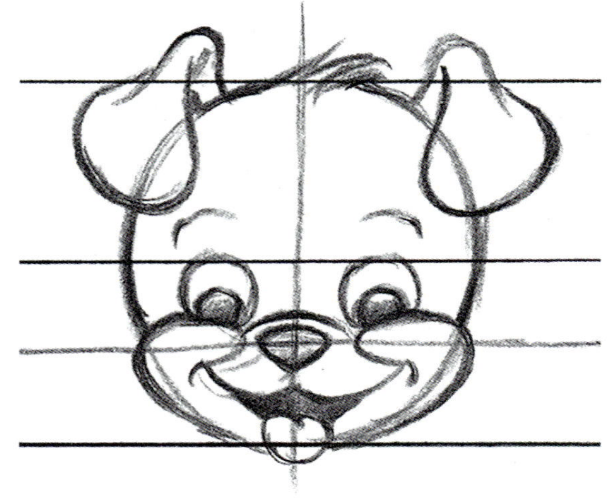

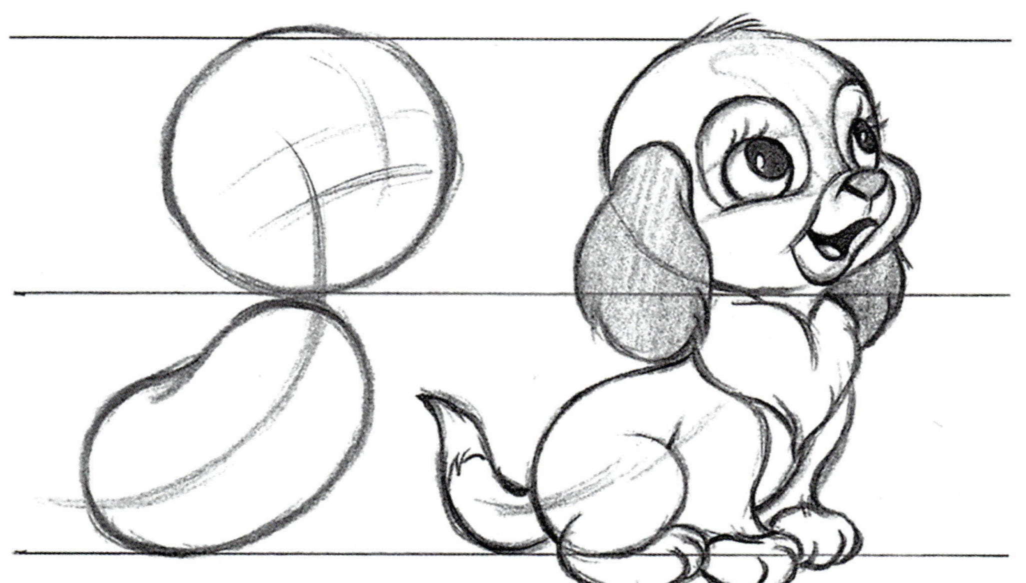

Creating a Full Figure
To construct a cute little animal, such as this pup, start with a body shaped like a plump bean. Add a circle for the head that has just about the same volume as the body.

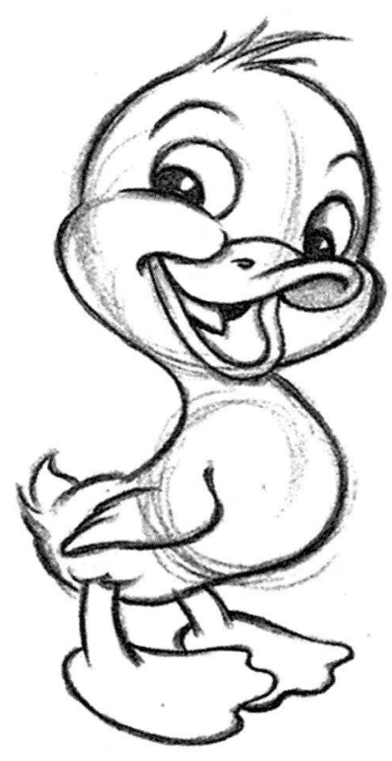

The Look
This wise quacker gives an engaging sidelong glance.

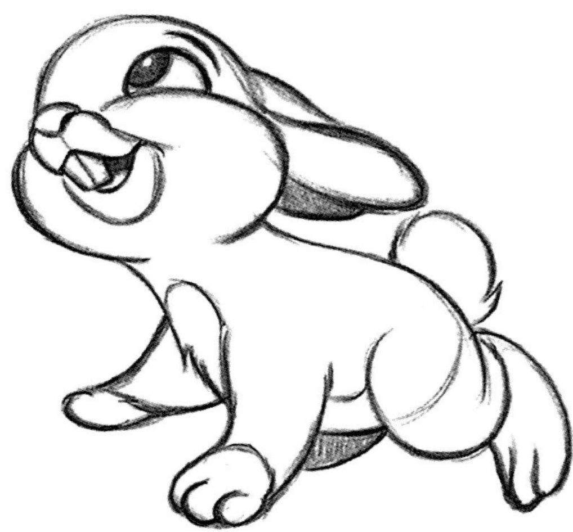

Body Language
This cuddly bunny looks up, emphasizing her small size and fragility. The tilt of the head and the springy stance add to the appeal.

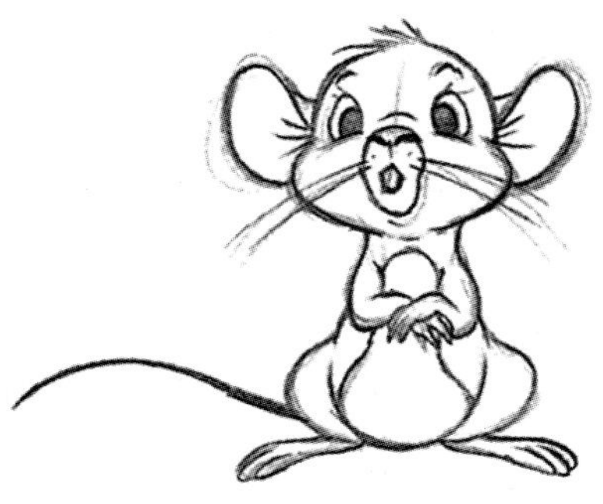

Nothing to Be Afraid Of
Tiny creatures with bright eyes and paws like hands, mice are among the most appealing cartoon animals.

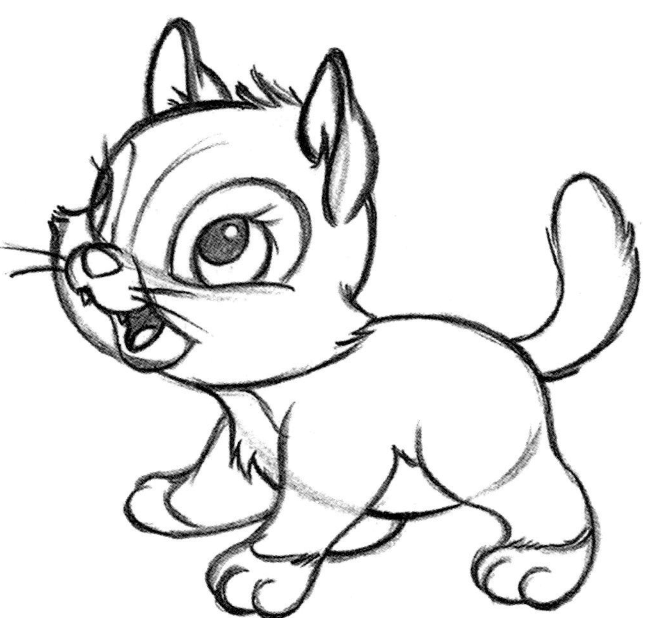

Playful as a Kitten
Notice the childlike proportions of this adorable kitten. The huge eyes give it an innocent expression.

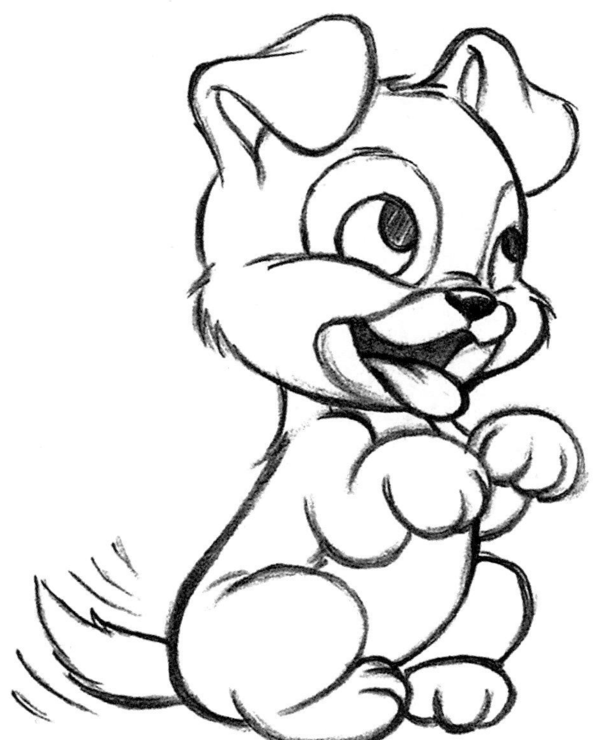

Begging to Be Loved
The wagging tail and visible tongue make this smiling pup look even happier.

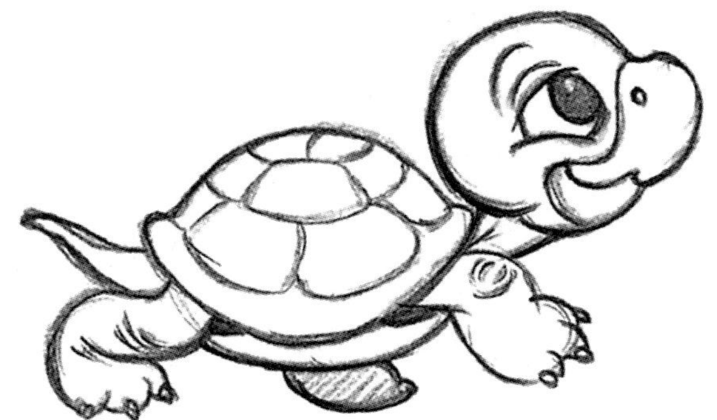

Real Details
The turtle's wrinkled knees and beaky face are realistic details that make this slowpoke believable.

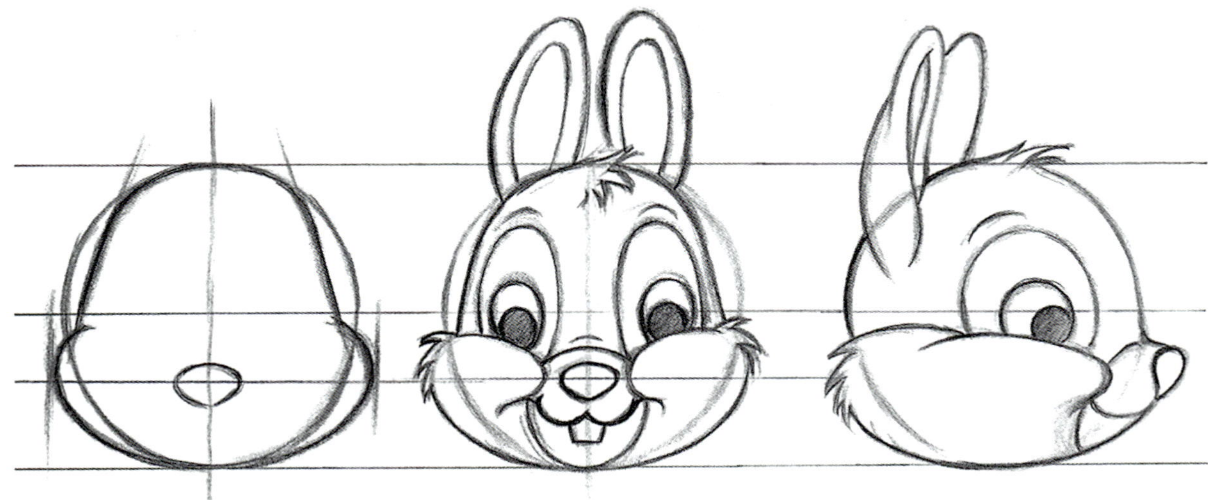

Variations on a Theme
Bunnies, squirrels, and chipmunks are drawn following the same formula, but bunnies have slightly larger cheeks and narrower foreheads. A bunny's eyes are set a little higher, but they still rest on the cheeks. Oversized front teeth add to the appeal.

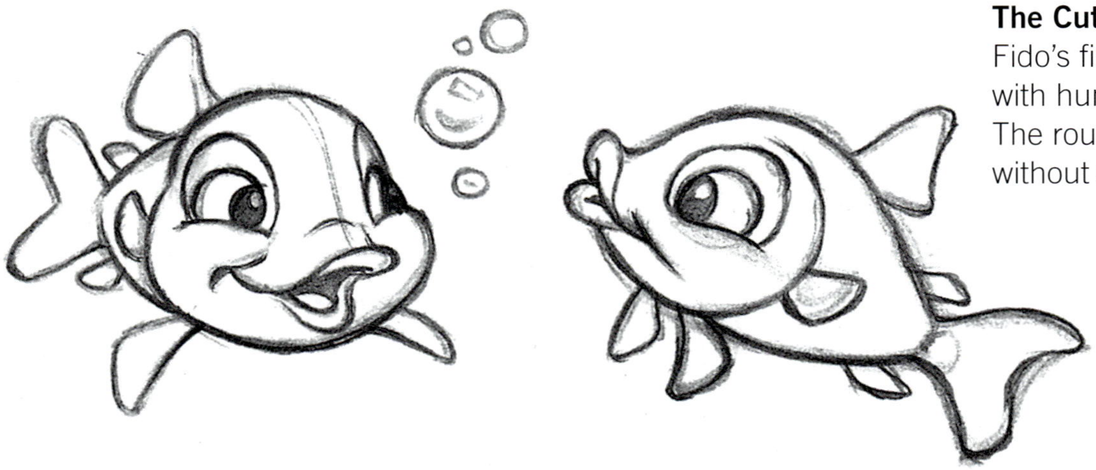

The Cute Treatment
Fido's finny friends have been "cutified" with human eyes and chubby cheeks. The rounded lips are suitably fishy without sacrificing a smile.

TIP

When drawing "cute" characters, keep the shading and details to a minimum.

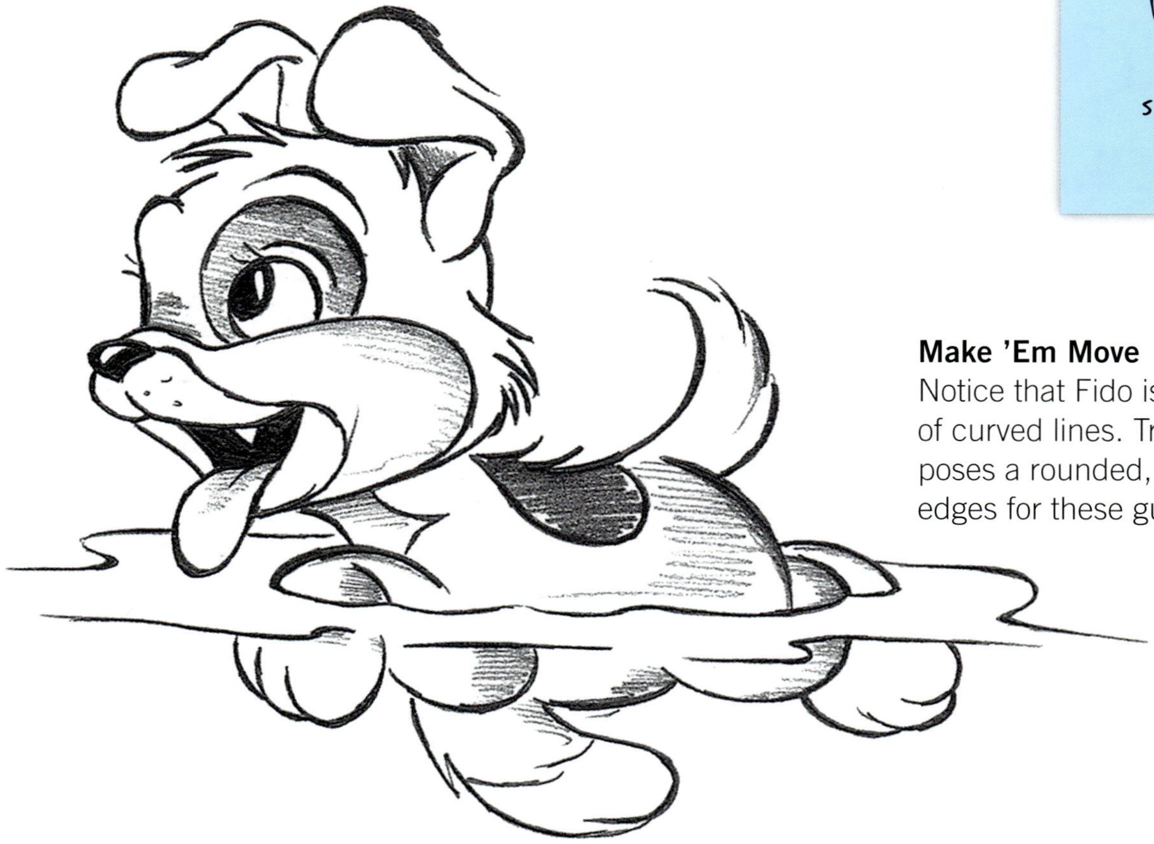

Make 'Em Move
Notice that Fido is made entirely of curved lines. Try to give action poses a rounded, fluid look. No hard edges for these guys.

About Face

You can start with a simple, ball-shaped head and spin off in many directions. Here we've started with a babyish head and a pair of round eyes and created a variety of cute animals by changing the ears, nose, and mouth. Add a tuft of hair, eyelashes, or maybe some whiskers to finish your own cartoon animal.

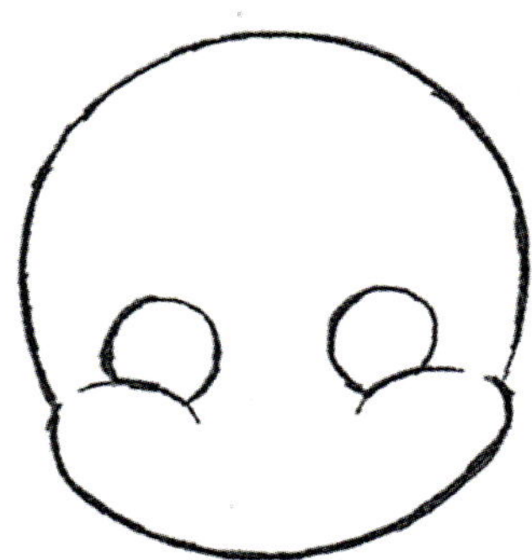

Start with a basic head shape based on a circle with chubby cheeks.

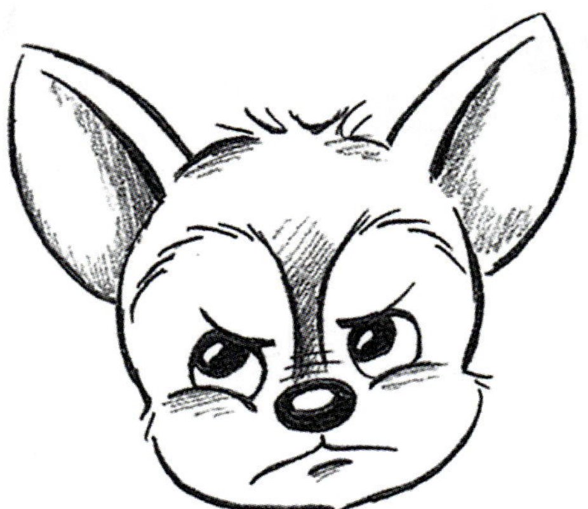

Downturned eyebrows and mouth let you know this pup's in a cranky mood.

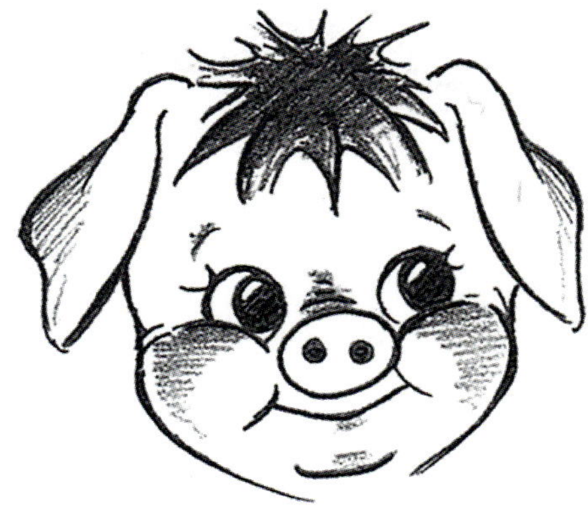

A softer jawline, plumper cheeks, and rounder nose are appropriate for a pig.

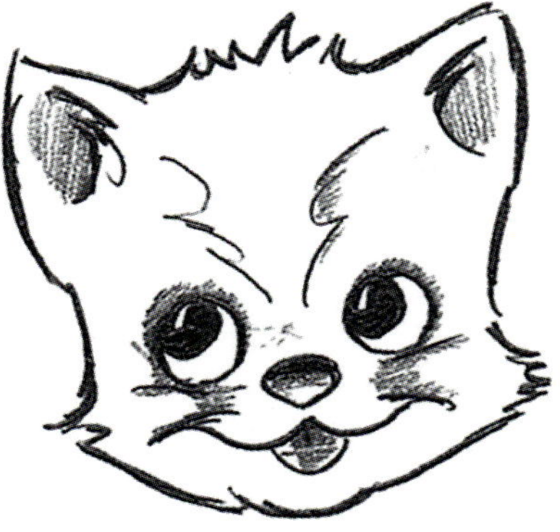

This kitten's mouth points up in the center, and its little nose points down.

THE HUMAN TOUCH

Giving animals human characteristics allows cute animals to stand in for people. These characters often wear clothes, drive cars, and live in houses. Their bodies become more human in proportion and yet retain some degree of animal identity.

Kid Proportions

Cute animal-people can be drawn with the same proportions as cute kids; both kittens here are 2½ heads high. The first kitten has button-eyed, graphic simplicity, and the second has saucer-shaped eyes and a wide, white muzzle.

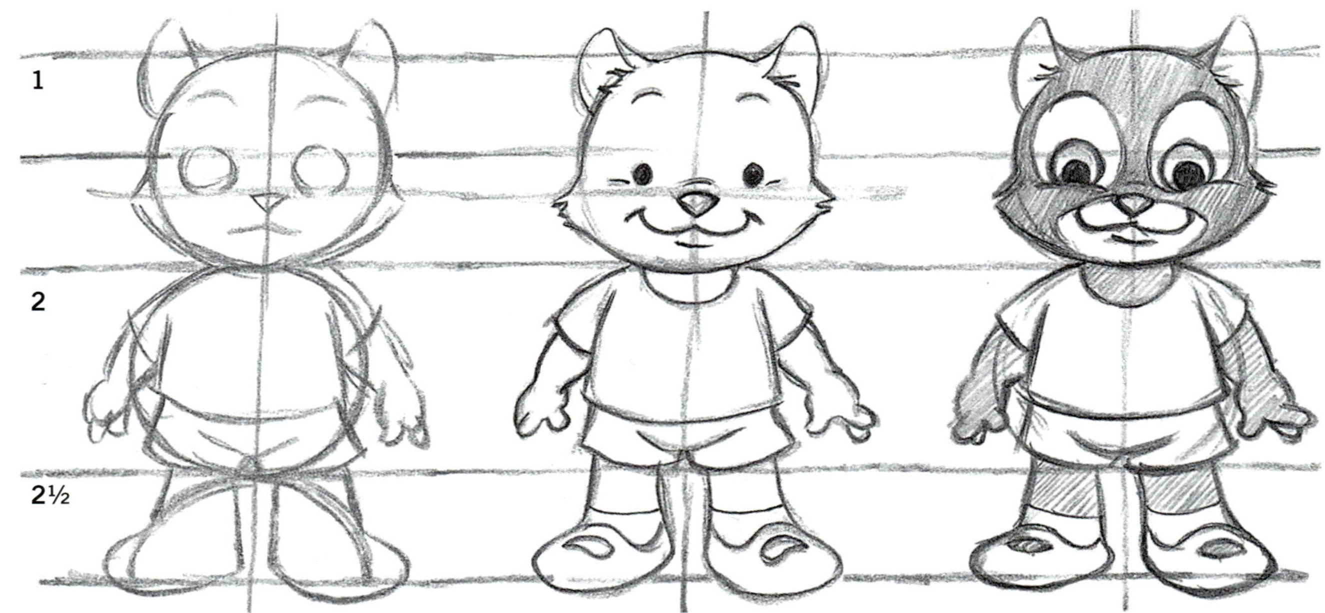

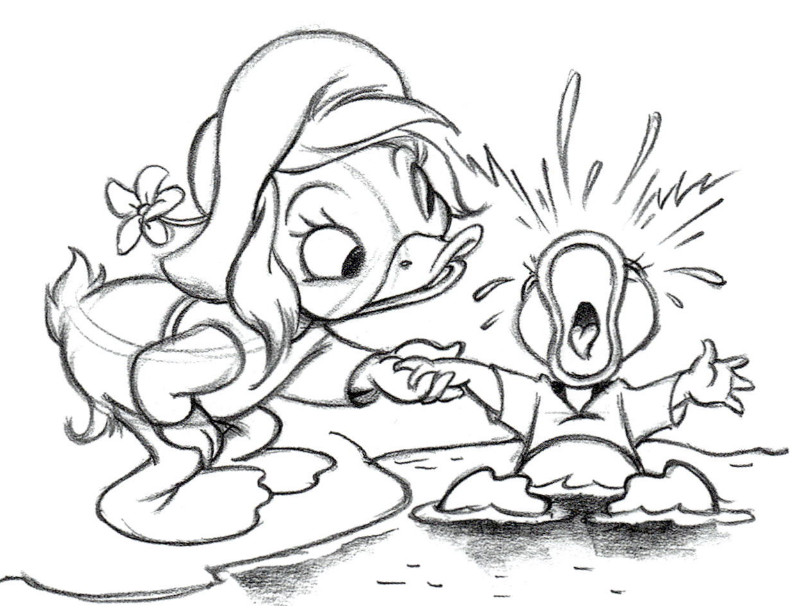

Waaaa!

Draw a few zigzag lines and teardrop shapes to show that this little duckling is howling up a storm. The wide-open mouth makes his attitude readily apparent, even though you can't see his eyes at all.

Cute as a Bug in a Rug

Insects are perennially popular cartoon creatures, and they pose unique design problems. How many legs do you draw? Do you give smiles and noses to bugs? What is the fashionable insect wearing this season? Stripes and polka dots are always "in," but it's up to you, pal.

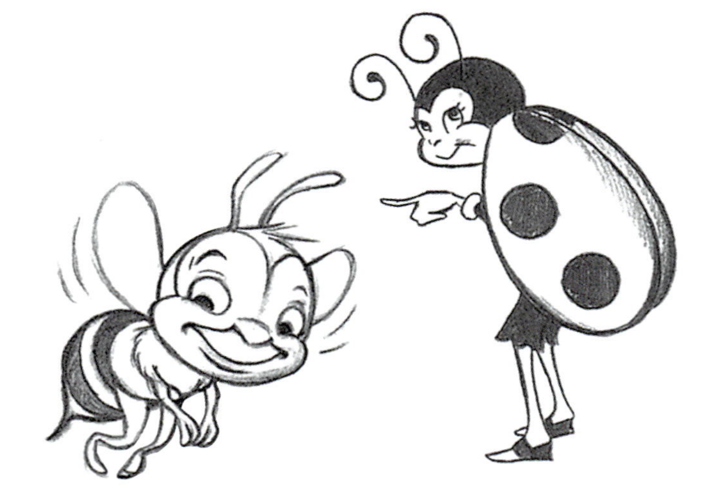

HANDS DOWN

On animal-people, paws become three- or four-fingered hands—small, pudgy, and cute. Keep the fingers short. For birds, make the feather fingers more tapered. Horses, pigs, and other animals with hooves present a challenge. You can draw hooves as gloved hands. Or draw them to look like hooves, but more flexible, like a hand inside a sock or mitten.

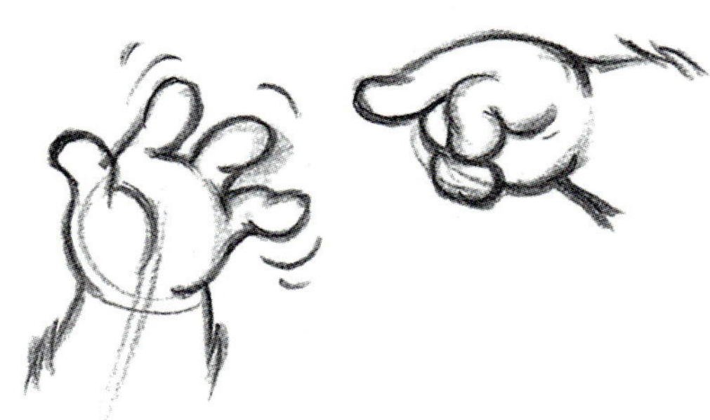

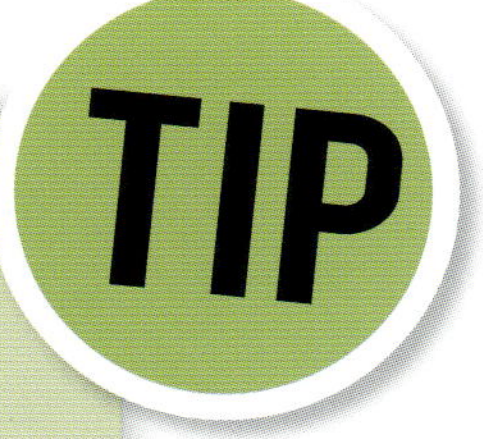

Keep animal poses lively and energetic. Giving youngsters a toe-in or toe-out stance keeps them from looking stiff and grown-up. Also, keep the number of toes to three or four and skip the toenails!

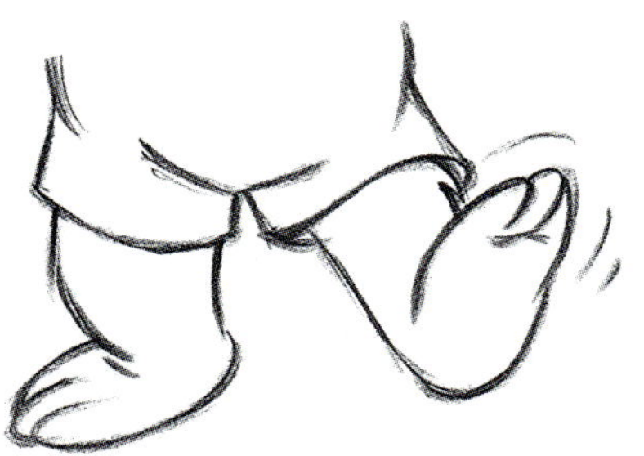

Bear Footed
Giving your bears bare feet is a cute alternative to drawing shoes—plus it makes the little guys seem vulnerable.

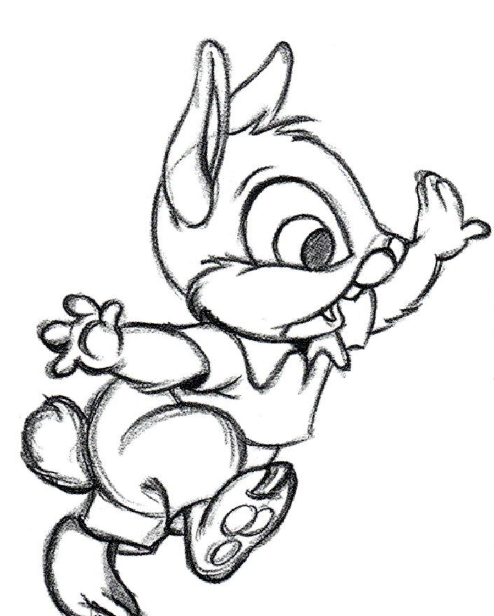

Happy Hopper
Bunny boy is drawn with kidlike proportions, outfit, and pose, but his padded feet remind you that he's really a rabbit in boy's clothing.

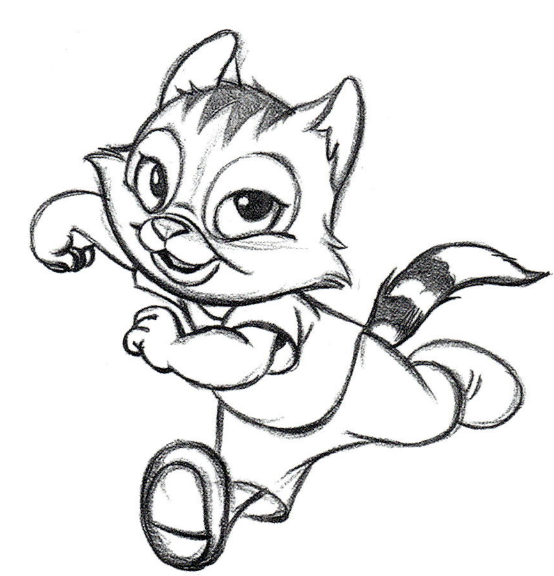

Shoe-In
Animal kids sometimes wear shoes. Keep them simple.

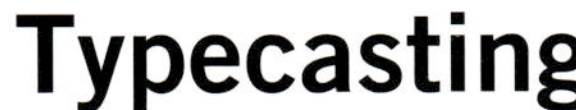

Typecasting

From the brave lion to the sly fox, animals have been used to embody human traits in stories from Aesop's fables to Saturday morning cartoons. You can effectively employ these stereotypes to allow people some immediate understanding of your character's personality. You can also get mileage out of turning stereotypes upside-down by drawing a fearless mouse or a speedy turtle.

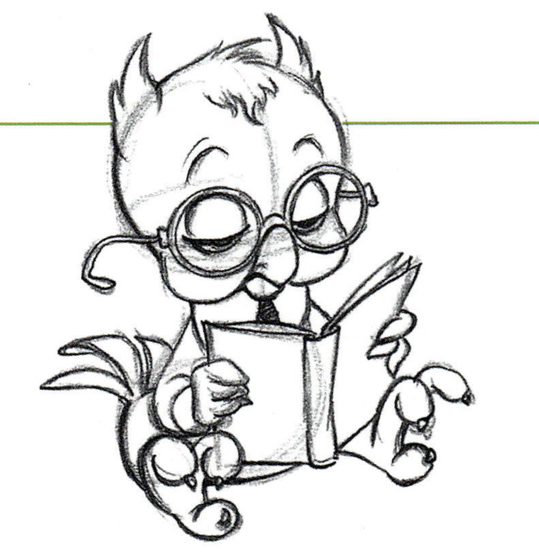

ZANY IS AS ZANY DOES

The zany character's mission is to look funny and do funny things. Everything about him is excessive. When he's scared, make him jump out of his skin—literally. Or make him melt into a puddle on a scorching hot day.

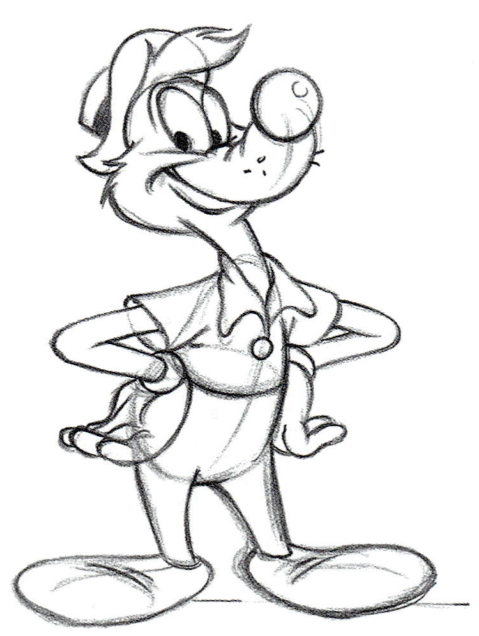

Hello!
Meet the typical, upstanding cartoon zany. He's a humanized animal with a pear-shaped body. Floppy ears would make him canine. You could also change him into a fox by adding pointy ears and a full fluffy tail.

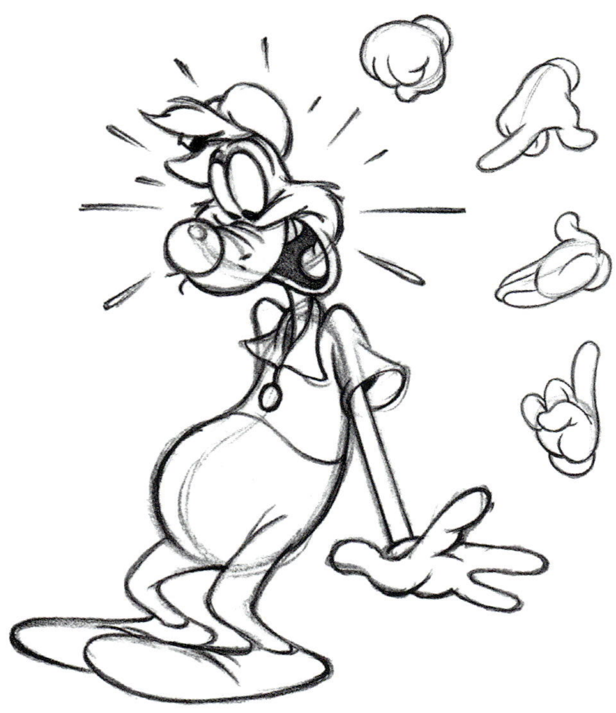

A Handy Guy
Our hero's arms and legs are like rubber hoses, and they can stretch for extreme action. Immense hands and feet render him clumsy and clownish. Four-fingered hands are easier to draw, and they allow for a full range of motion.

Zany Expressions

This loudmouth was drawn with an undersized cranium. The lower part of his face is wide to accommodate a big mouth and a bulbous nose. His eyes are close together with beady pupils and eyelids that fly up in astonishment and scrunch down in anger. Tremendous, rubbery features broadcast emotions quickly.

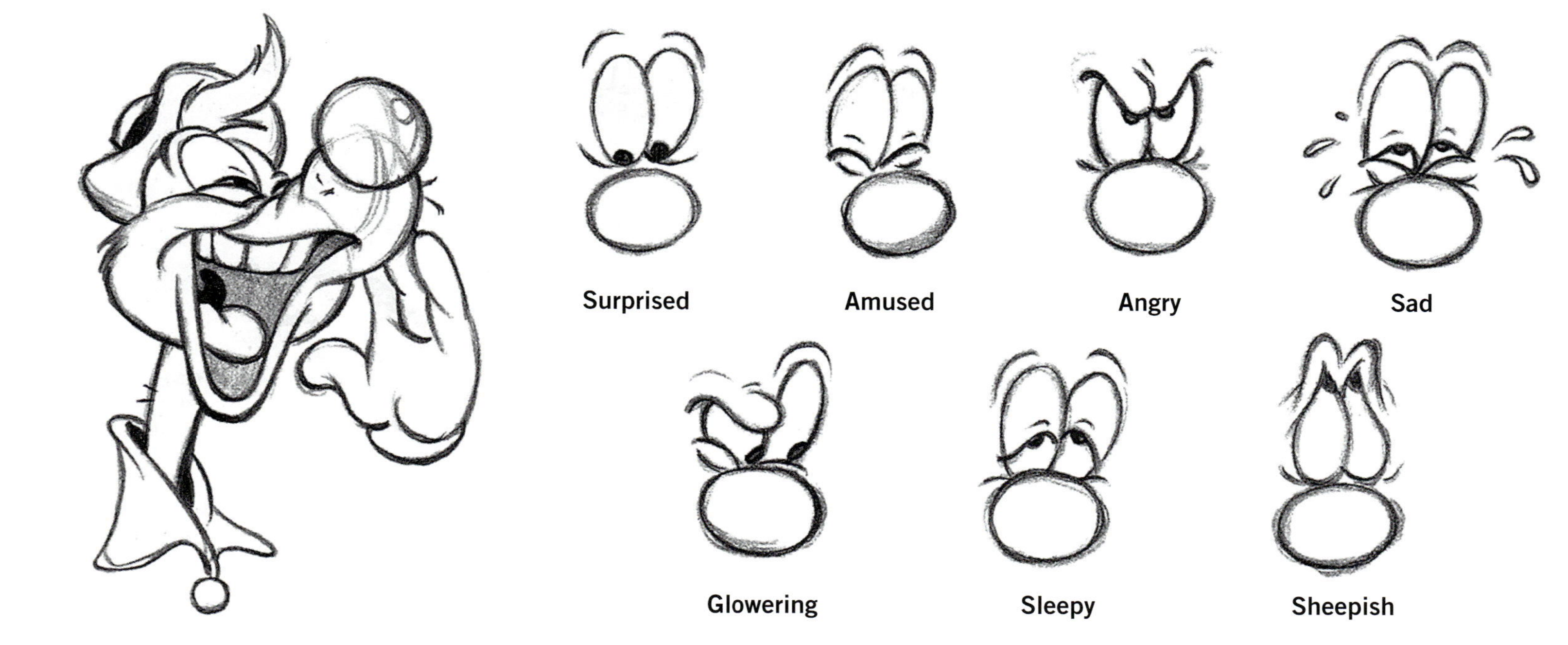

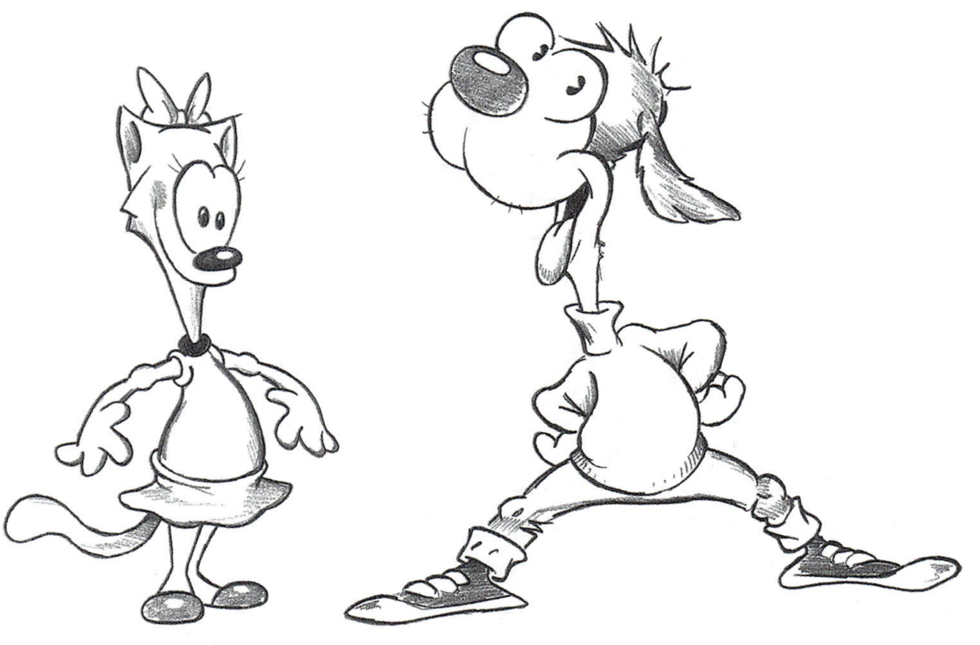

Stretching It

Enormous google eyes, teardrop-shaped bodies, and silly attitudes are among the elements that link this goofy dog and cat couple.

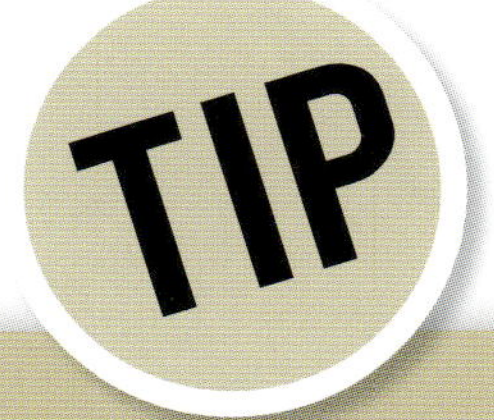

Think out the logic behind your animal zanies. It usually doesn't make sense to mix humans and dressed-up animals unless you have a reason. However, that rule can be broken if you do so intentionally.

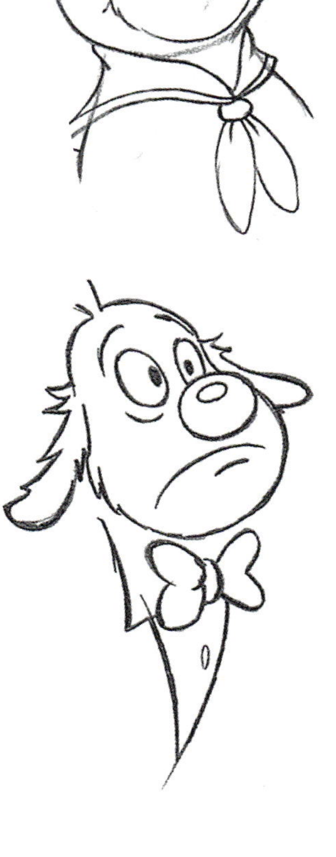

Grouping 'Em

Give your gang a consistent look. These characters have individual personalities, but because they're designed with a pear-shaped head and simple, rounded features, they work well as a group.

Big Bully

The thuggish features of a big bulldog make for an ideal bully. Putting him in a uniform can be even funnier. The size relationships among characters can accent the action.

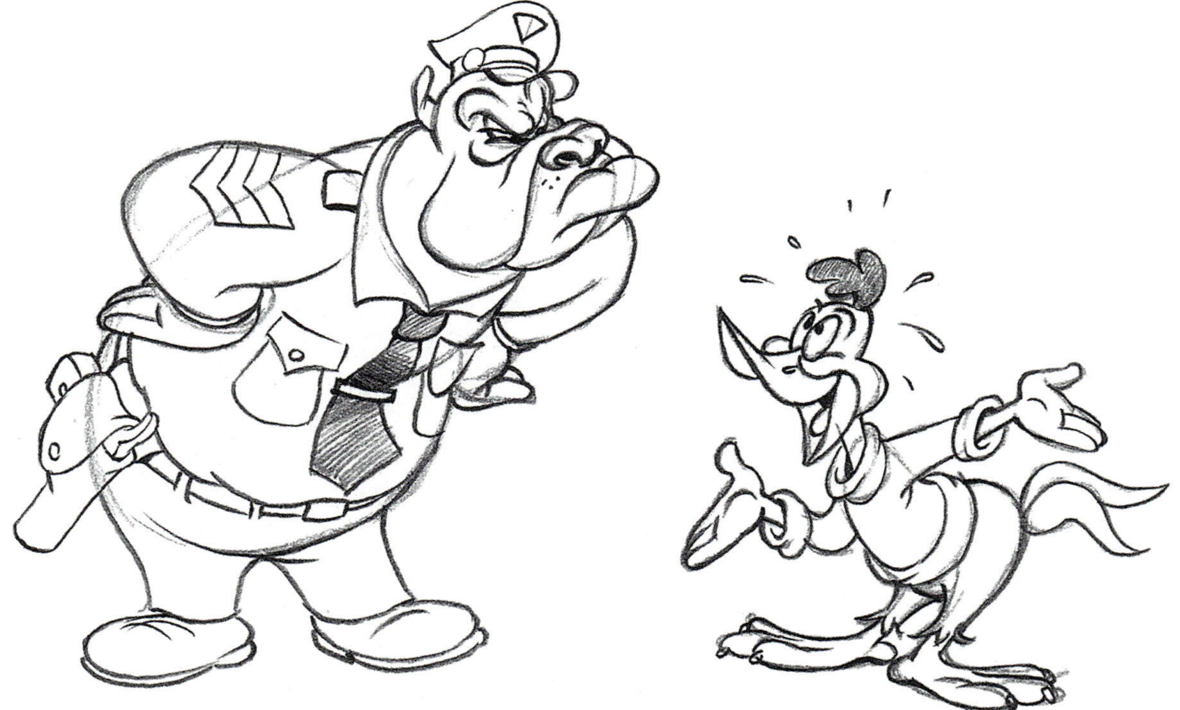

CRAZY CHARACTERS

By emphasizing the characteristics your fellow humans display, you'll find that you have a wealth of satiric material to work with. Exaggeration and simplification are the keys. A receding hairline becomes a shiny dome, dreamy eyes are as large as saucers, and a smattering of freckles becomes five or six polka dots.

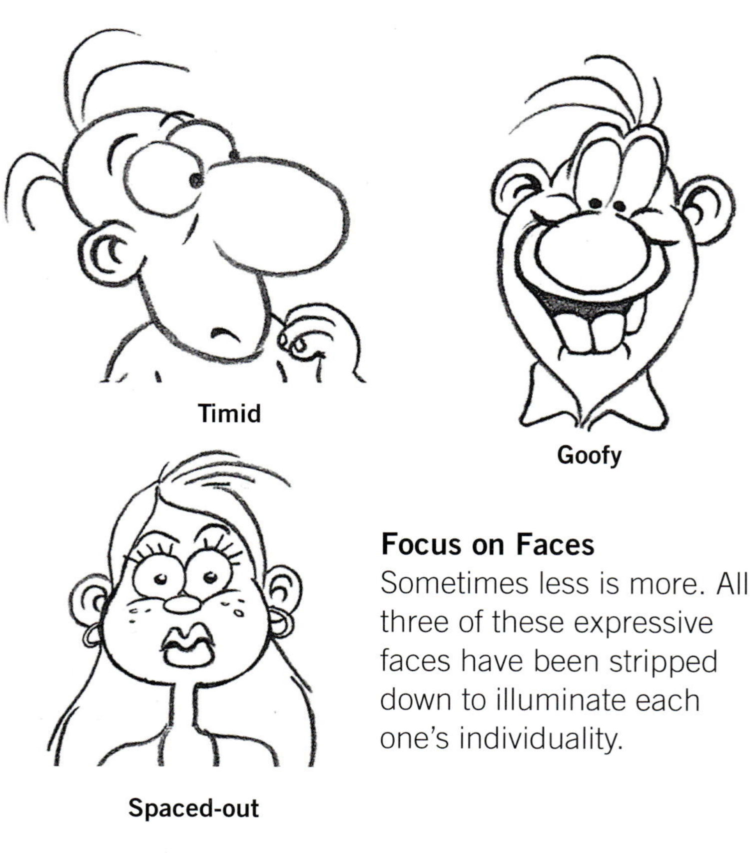

Timid

Goofy

Spaced-out

Focus on Faces
Sometimes less is more. All three of these expressive faces have been stripped down to illuminate each one's individuality.

Suits Me
Give your character a body and clothing. A simple character doesn't need a fussy outfit—especially if he's out for a jog. And a simple doughnut shape and trouser silhouette is enough to suggest a turtleneck sweater and shoes for a dog lover.

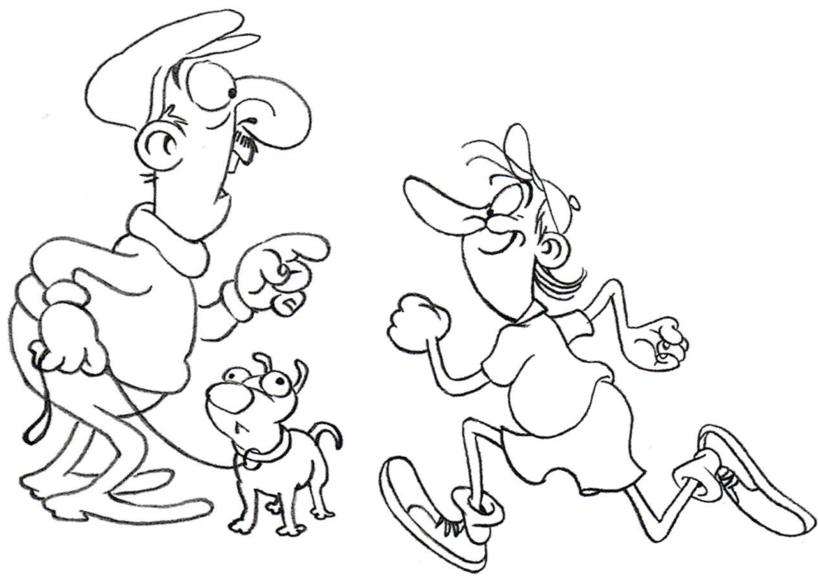

The Nose Knows
Here's a good way to spark some ideas. Quickly sketch a variety of possible cartoon head shapes. Pear and sausage shapes make good skulls for cartoon zanies. Then stick a wacky nose on each of the heads. Now, what comes to mind? An artsy witch? A silly sailor?

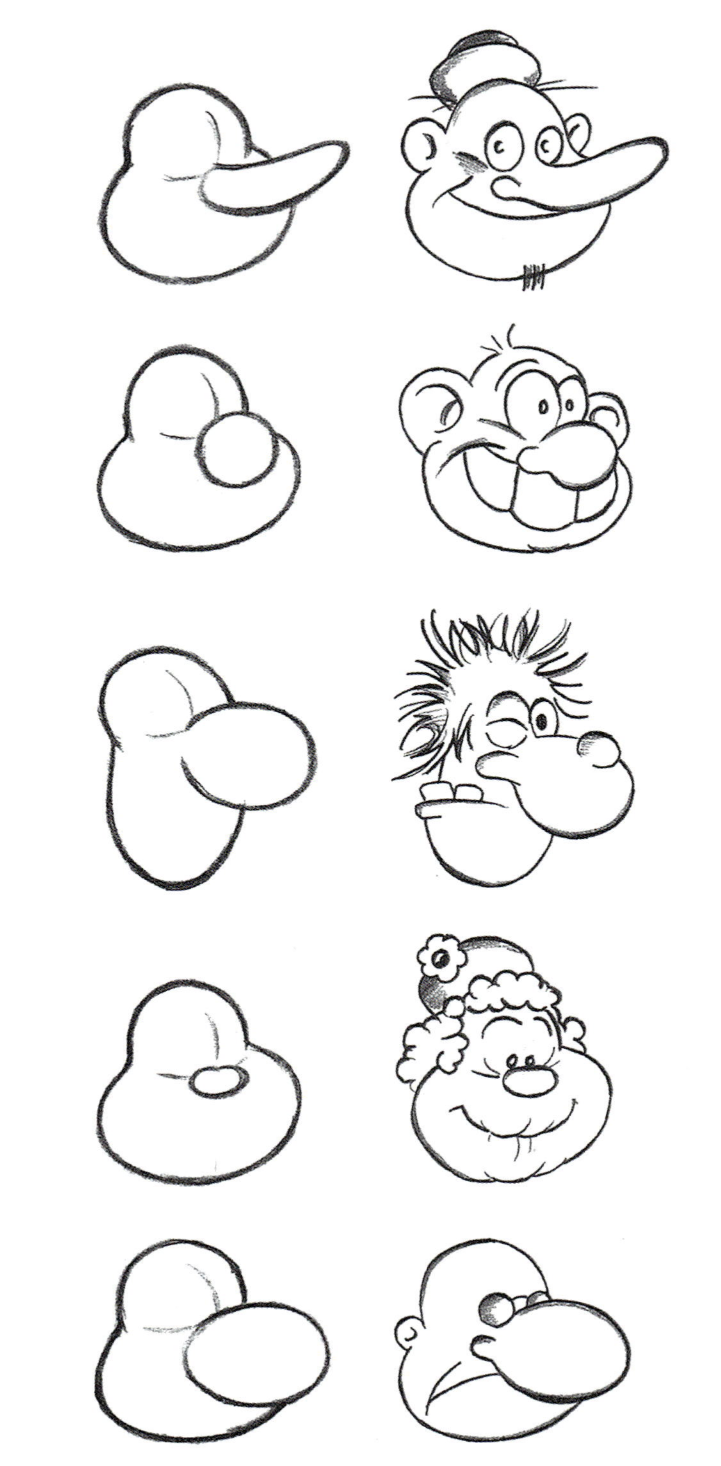

GETTING A GRAPHIC START

These drawings have been created using as few lines as possible. Notice what is missing in these drawings. Insignificant details have been omitted. Positive and negative areas can be used to great effect in black and white cartoons. The dark shape of a vest or jacket gives weight and anchors the drawing. This can be particularly effective when contrasted with a thin, whimsical line.

Go Picasso

The design of comic characters can be influenced by abstract art. Why not put both eyes on the same side of the head? Feel free to be as wacky as you wanna be.

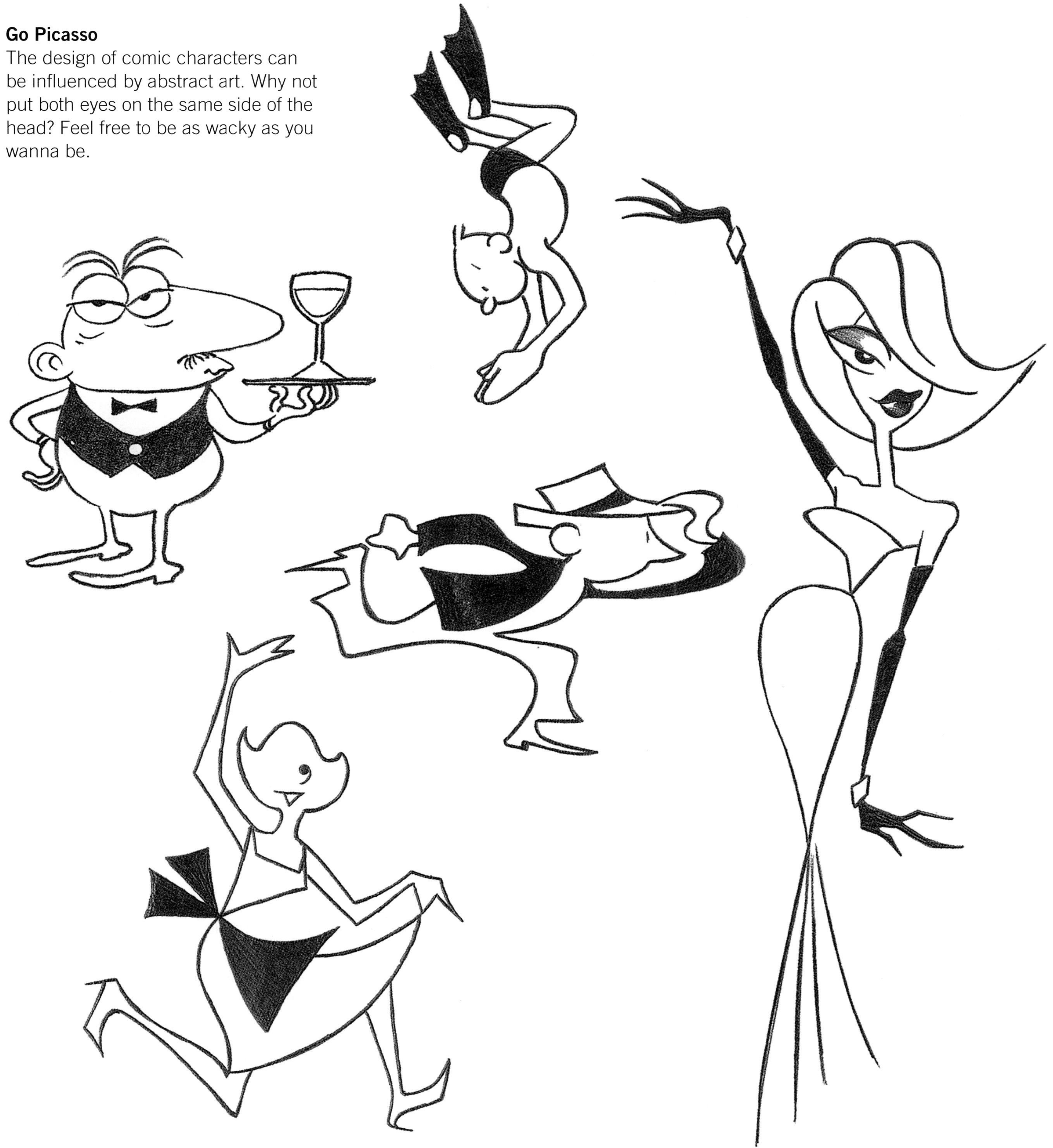

CRITTER CRAZY

One trick for drawing cartoon animals is to think of them as an assembly of simple shapes, like globes, sausages, pears, and eggs. By playing off the natural colors and markings of your animal characters, you can have critters who are spotted, striped, and wildly colored, adding to the visual excitement.

EXAGGERATE!

The bulldog wildly barking at a mailman or the hairy ape mimicking human behavior provide ample opportunity for the kind of squashed and stretched facial expressions and slapstick antics that are the basis of zany cartoon humor. Lumpish camels, fat pigs, and contented cows have funny faces and peculiar body shapes that give you plenty of material to work with.

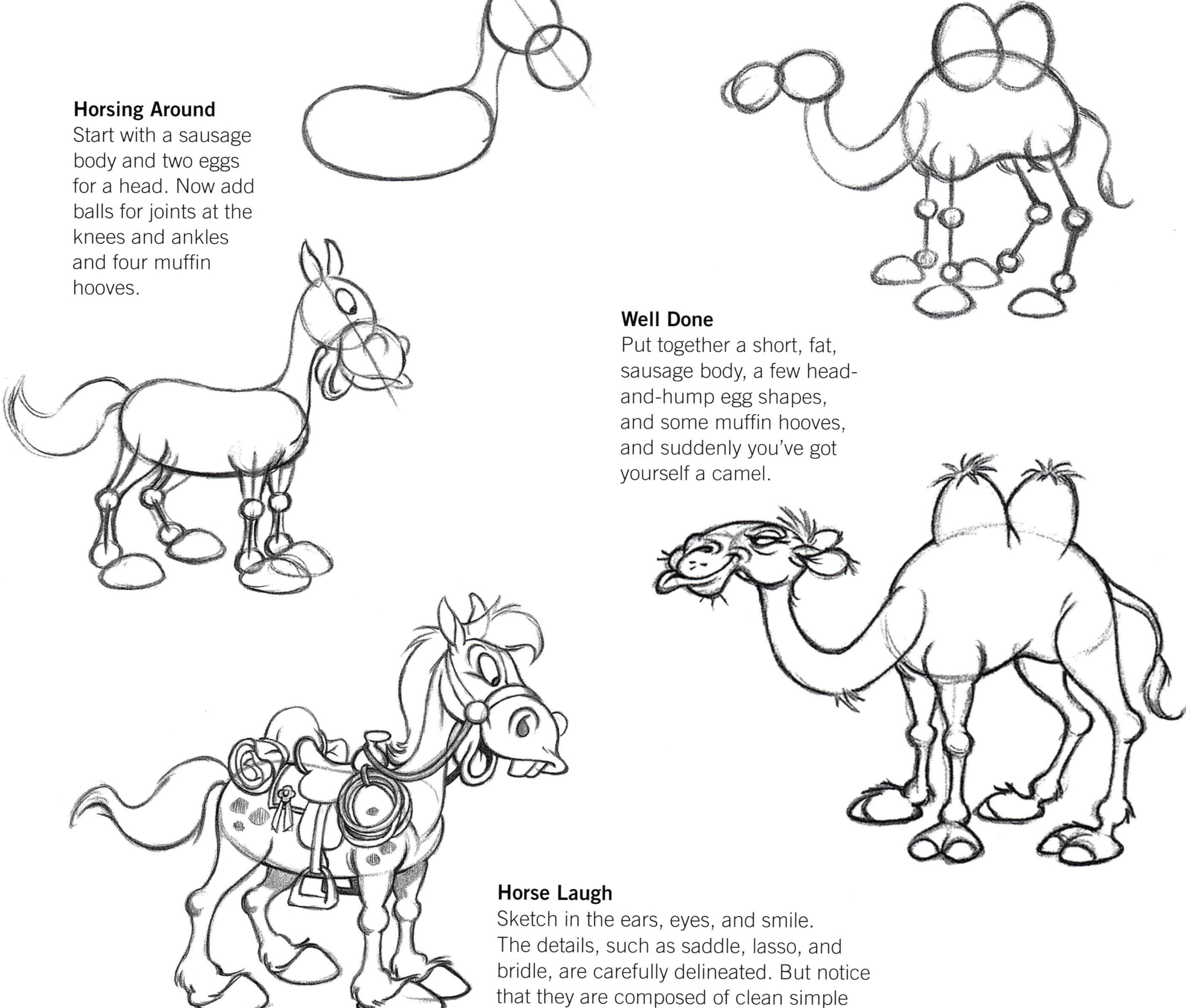

Horsing Around
Start with a sausage body and two eggs for a head. Now add balls for joints at the knees and ankles and four muffin hooves.

Well Done
Put together a short, fat, sausage body, a few head-and-hump egg shapes, and some muffin hooves, and suddenly you've got yourself a camel.

Horse Laugh
Sketch in the ears, eyes, and smile. The details, such as saddle, lasso, and bridle, are carefully delineated. But notice that they are composed of clean simple shapes. Saddle up!

RUBBER LEGS

The animals on this page all share a sausage body and have long hoses for legs. Their rubbery limbs make them look flexible, fluid, and funny. Big clodhopper feet add to the clumsy, comic effect.

What Was That?

Can you picture your characters turning in space? As Fido spins around to watch Jack Rabbit flash by, the soft folds of his jowls flap to the side. This is the "wave principle" in action. To envision how a character might look from different angles, take a plastic cartoon doll and notice how it looks as you angle it in different directions, from profile to three-quarter to full-face views.

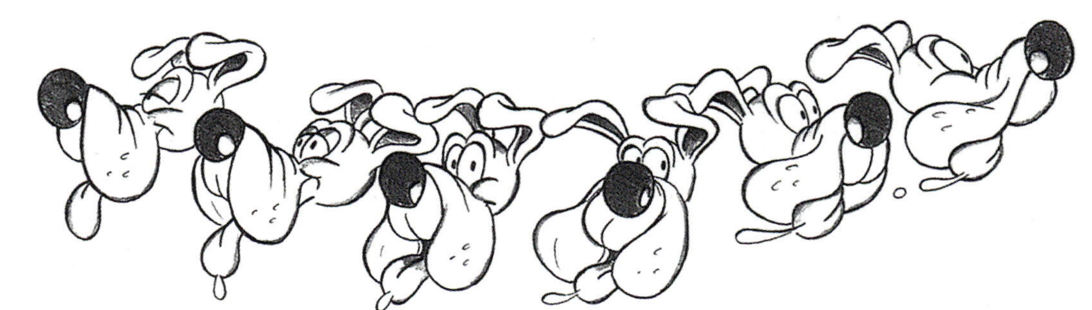

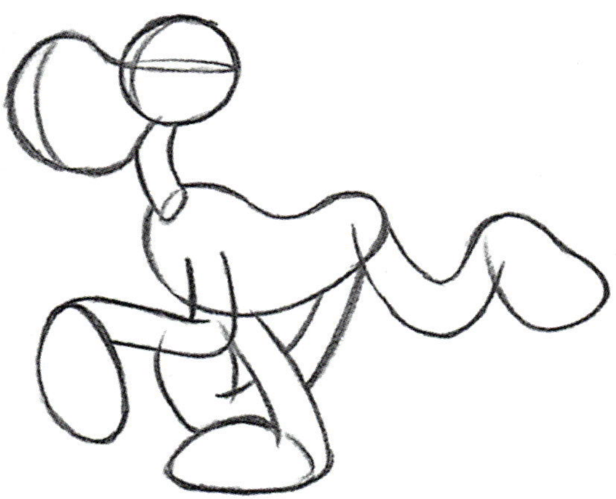

Similar Skeletons

Sketch out the basic shape of the body; then add the details—ears, tail, and nose—that make the character unique.

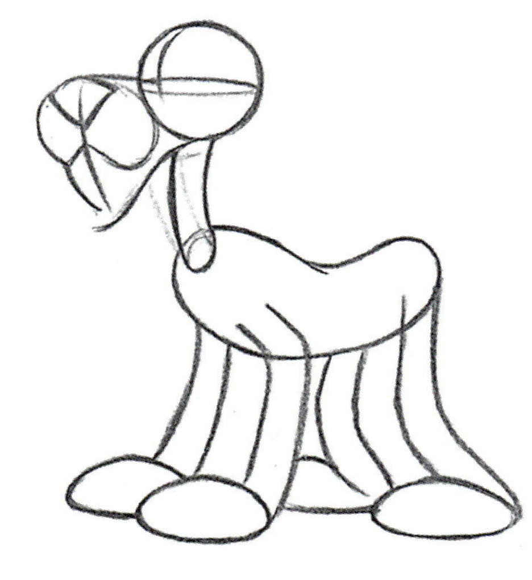

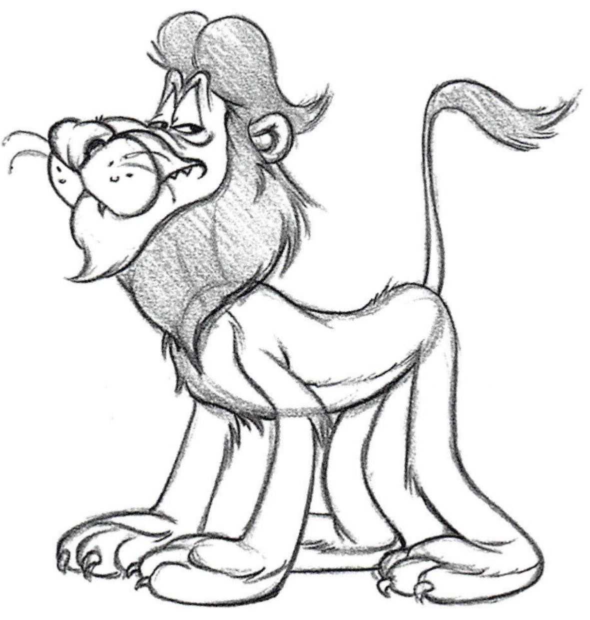

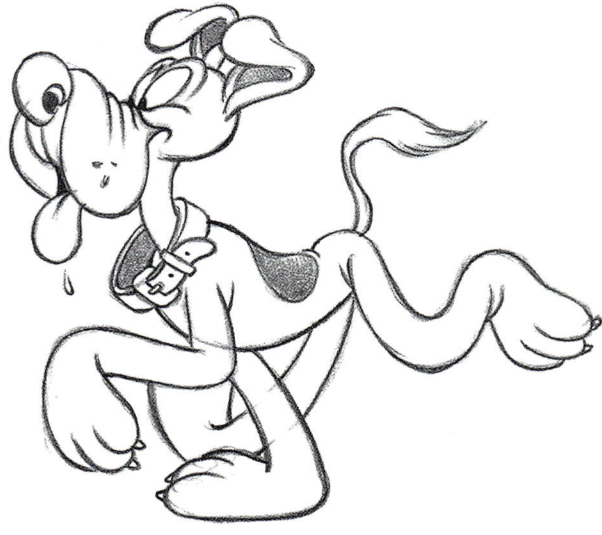

Flap-Jawed

Big-nosed, dreamy Fido is a jowly, drooling good ol' boy. His floppy ears and oversized collar accentuate the goofiness of this harmless clown.

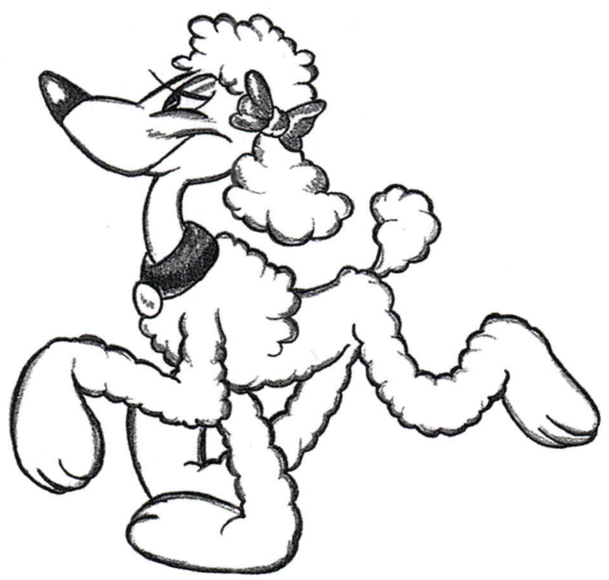

Très Chic

Fido and Fifi share the same canine construction used to very different effects. Flirty, long-lashed eyes, a pert, pointed nose, and soft lines combine to make this poodle fetching and feminine, though still funny.

GET REAL

Superhero stories, science fiction, and fantasy tales combine elements of reality with humor and make-believe. A somewhat more realistic approach is often called for to make these yarns seem plausible. This is a little bit more complicated than other types of cartooning. Knowledge of anatomy and perspective is required.

HEAD START

A good way to get started in this arena is by drawing faces. It's important to draw them well, as cartooning relies heavily on closeups. Try using a photograph for reference. Study it for the basic pose, and trace or copy it. Simplify and stylize your photographic image to develop a cartoon character.

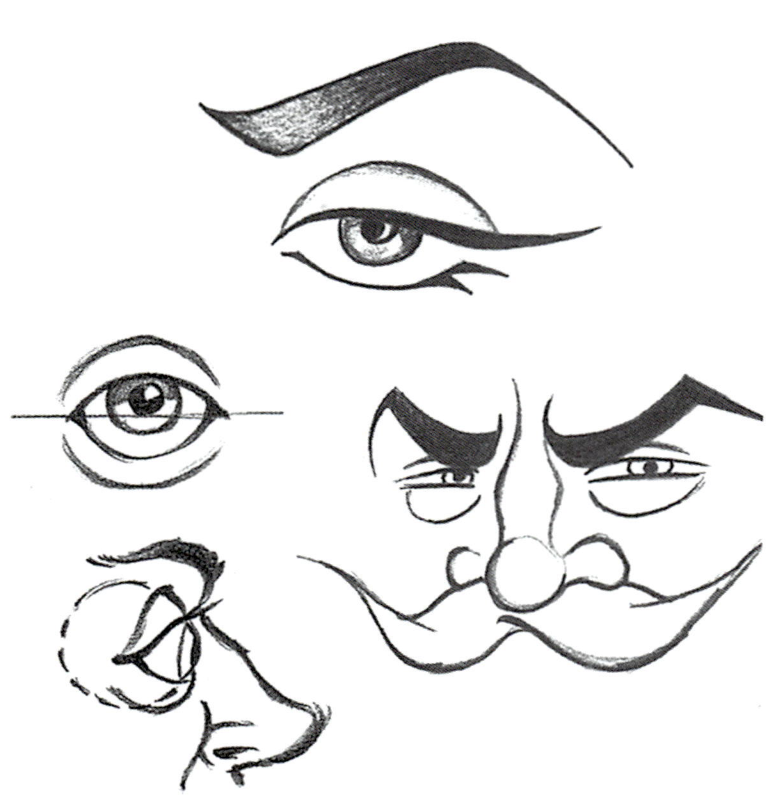

An Eye for an Eye
Think of the eye as a ball that has a lid above and a pouch below. You see only part of it—never the full circle at one time. And with an icy stare, a startled look, or a sultry glance, the eyes can be a barometer of emotion. What you reveal depends on the shape of the lid and the arch of the brow.

Making Headway

Skulls are almost always about the same shape in real life. In cartoons, you can start out with a naturalistic oval as a guideline or play with any other shape that strikes your fancy.

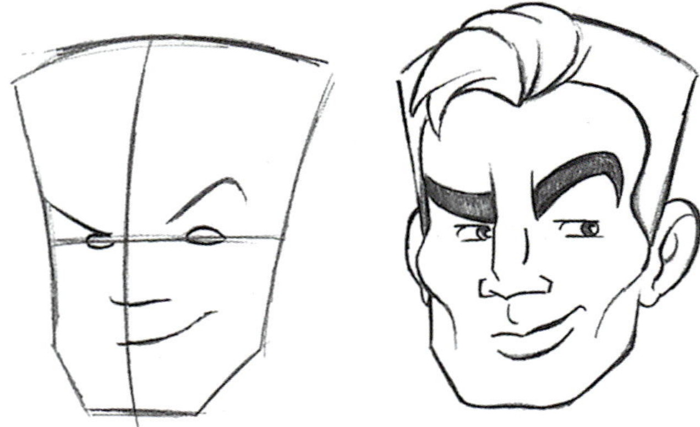

Rectangle Heroic Hank's head is a modified rectangle. Emphasize the strong jawline to give him a rugged look.

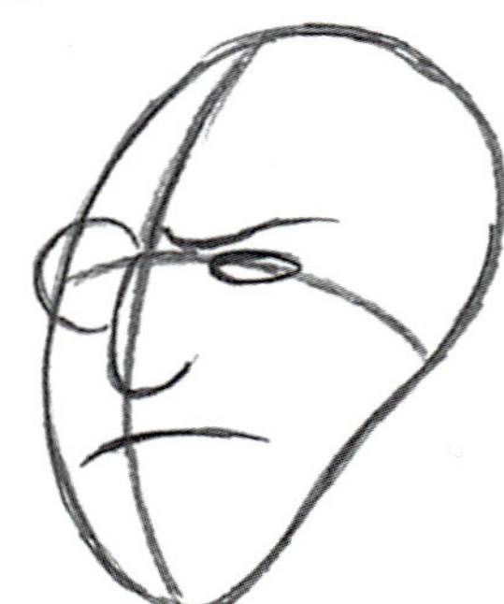
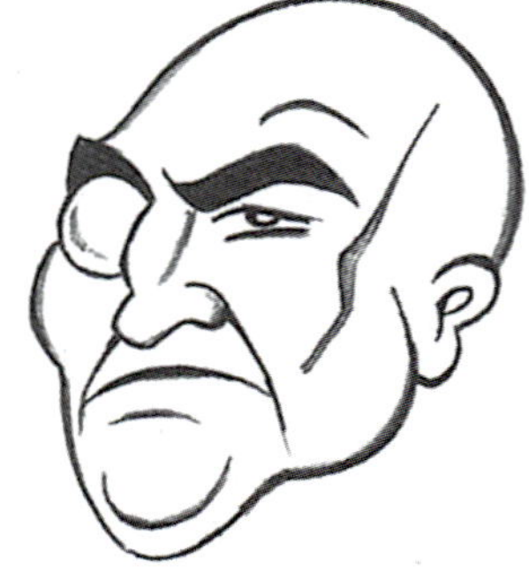

Kidney Bean A pointy bean-shape serves as a start for sour Uncle Otto. The downward curves accentuate his dour demeanor.

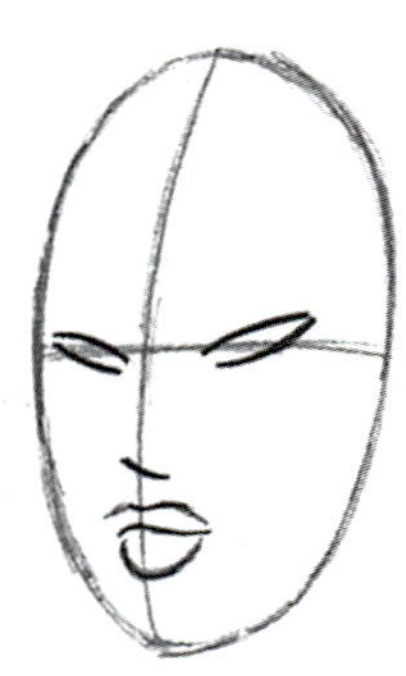
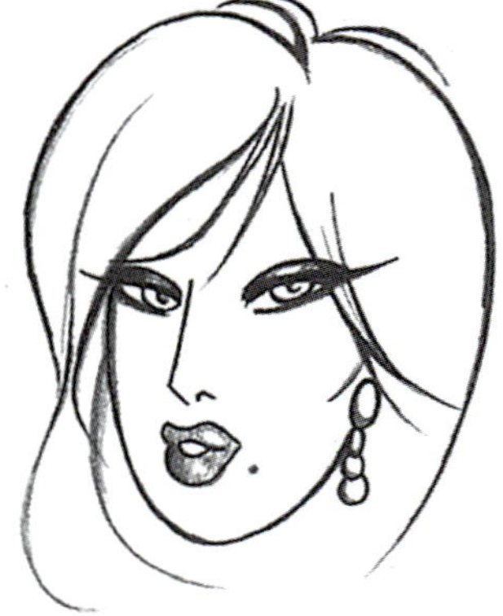

Oval Stylish Stella started out as a soft oval. With drawings of women, the shapes are often more rounded and elastic.

FACE OFF

Faces offer endless variety for the cartoonist. They can be angular and deeply furrowed or as round and soft as a water balloon. Eyes can be wide with wonder or narrowed in suspicion. A nose can be a baby button or strongly arched with flaring nostrils. The faces on this page suggest a variety of personalities.

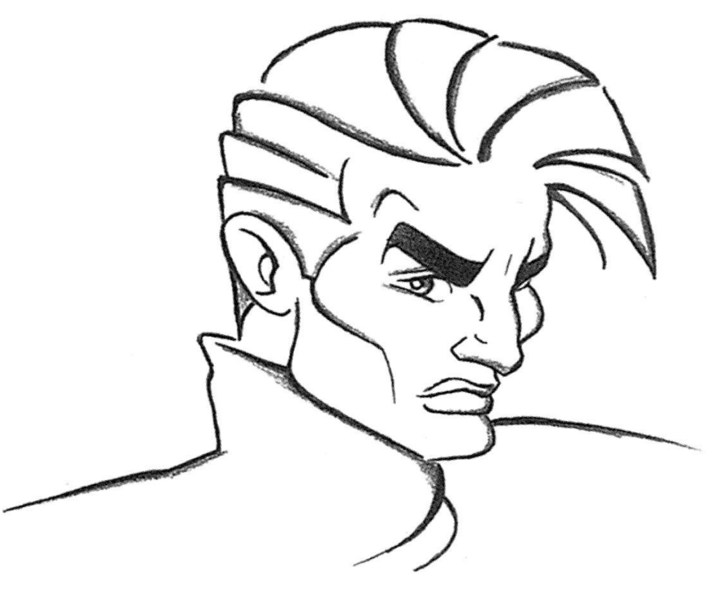

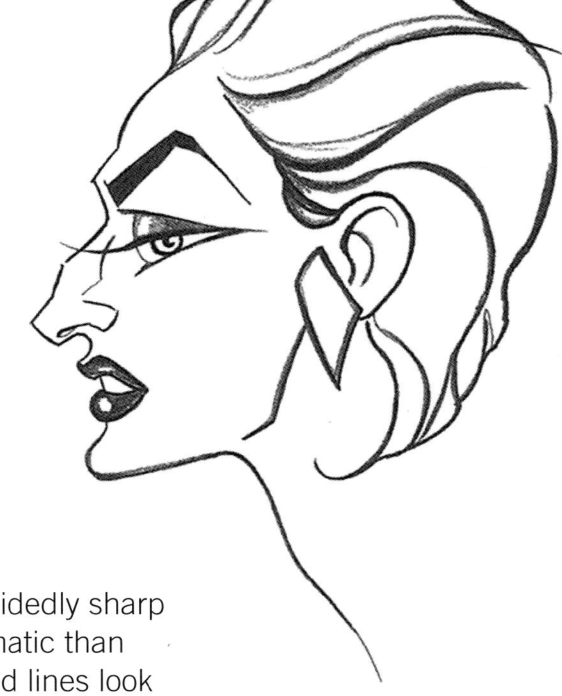

Villains

Arched brows over ice-cold eyes, lips curled in mockery, and a decidedly sharp sense of style often make villains appear more glamorous and dramatic than heroes. Remember that rounded forms are for softies. Sharp, jagged lines look far more dangerous. When drawing evil characters, emphasize strong facial structures, hard cheekbones, and severe expressions to make them look like lean and hungry scoundrels.

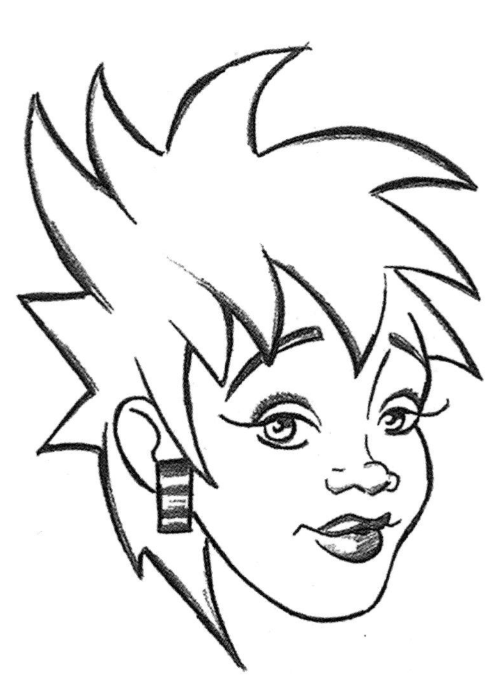

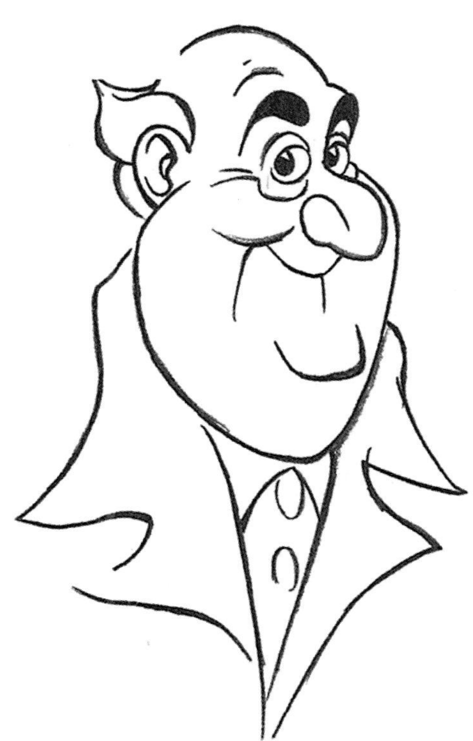

Heroes

Heroes in cartoons are usually conventionally attractive, with square jaws and strong cheekbones. A spiky haircut, a streak of white through a head of black hair, or a dramatic eyepatch can add individuality and hint at a darker side.

Soft Touch

This kindhearted fellow is anything but hard and heroic-looking. Draw the basic structure of the head and then fill out the lower half, leaving only a hint of a chin. Rounded curves under the eyes, full cheeks, and a simpering mouth add to the effect of softness.

BODY BUILDING

The next logical step after drawing faces is to tackle the whole figure. Taking a life-drawing class can be helpful, but you can also just grab your sketchbook and park yourself on a park bench. Knock out quick sketches of kids, joggers, and dog walkers. Gesture drawings are a great way to get a feel for poses and anatomy.

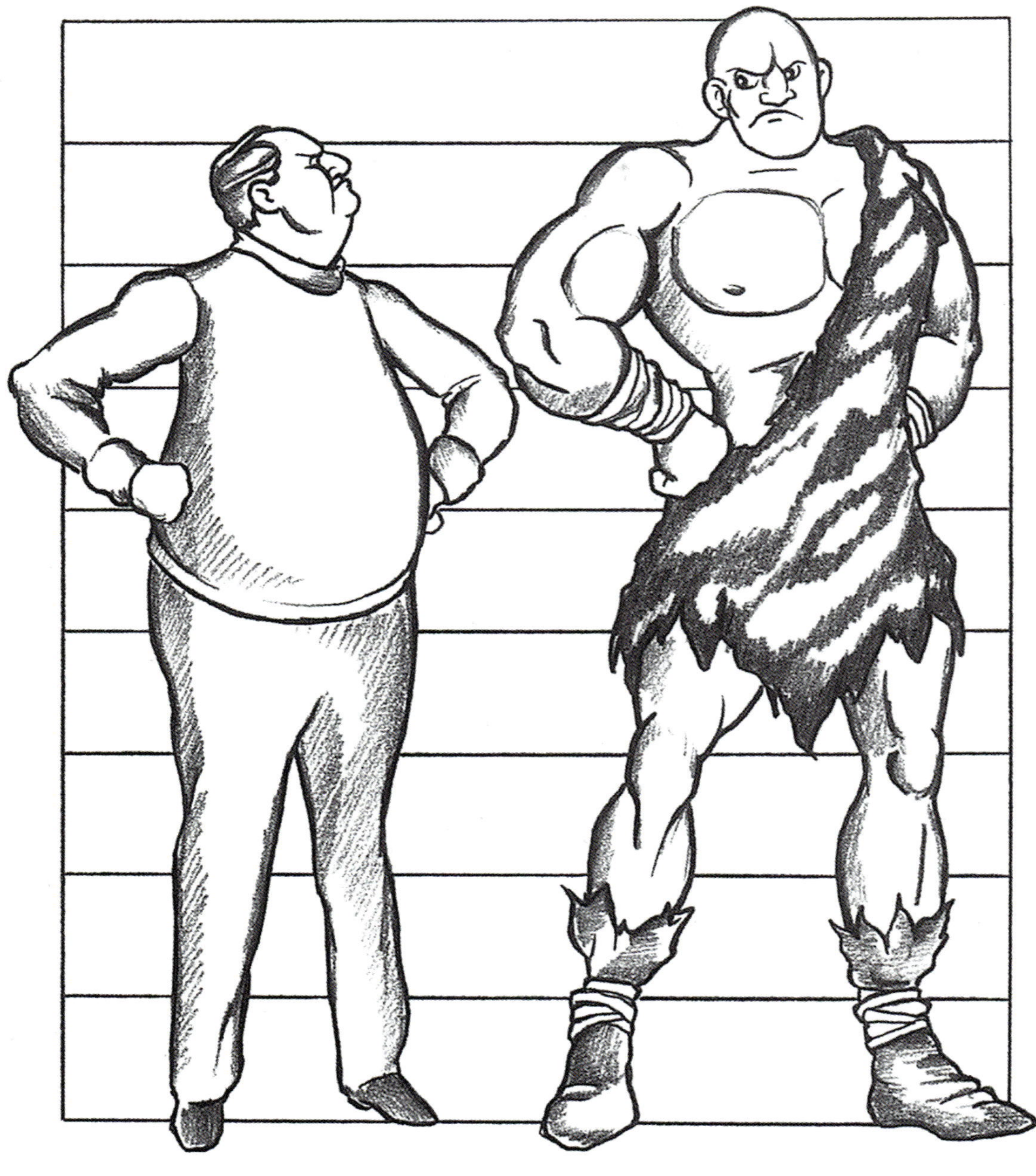

Heads Up

The human body is measured in heads for artistic purposes. The ideal form is about 8 heads high. Cartoonists and fashion illustrators exaggerate this proportion frequently. Superheroes, monsters, and evil mutants are often 9 or more heads tall, giving them a massive, imposing appearance.

If you want a model who never gets tired, buy a poseable wooden mannequin at an art supply store.

MOVE IT

Quick gesture drawings give you a sense of how the body moves in space. Start with a stick figure. This is the cartoon's skeleton, and it defines the pose and general proportions. The backbone is the line of action determining the stance and energy the figure will have. Remember that a backbone is flexible, and so is your pencil line. Depending on the curve you give, the figure can seem rigid with attention, curving and willowy, or drooping with exhaustion. Flesh it out with rounded shapes to suggest a large chest and small hips. Then reverse it, drawing the same stick figure, but with a small chest and large hips.

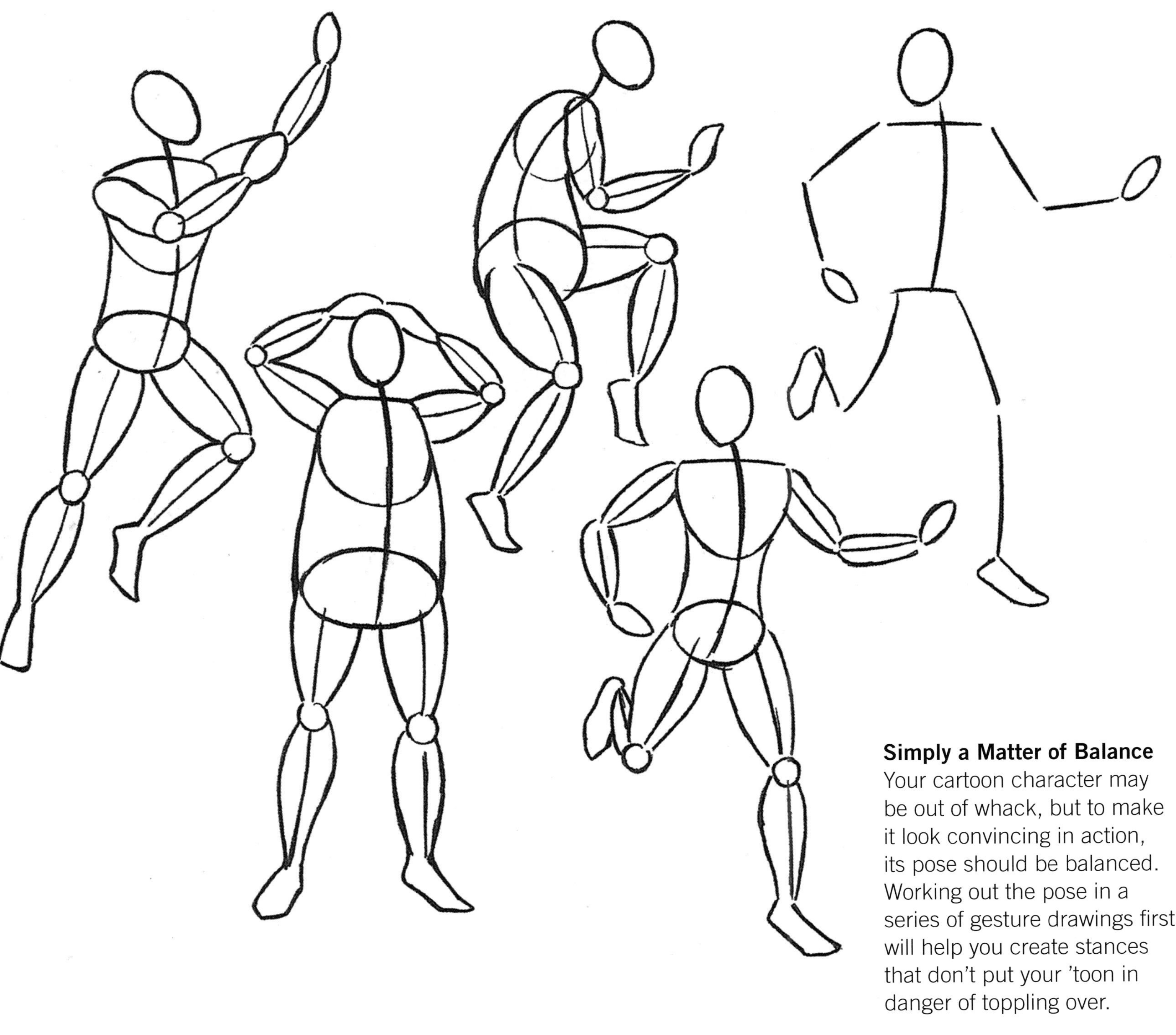

Simply a Matter of Balance
Your cartoon character may be out of whack, but to make it look convincing in action, its pose should be balanced. Working out the pose in a series of gesture drawings first will help you create stances that don't put your 'toon in danger of toppling over.

BUILDING BLOCKS

The best way to do anything complicated is to divide the job into simpler stages. To build a house, you start with the foundation, then add the walls and roof. You wouldn't start with the roof and work your way down to the ground. To ensure that your finished drawing is not out of proportion (unless you want it to be), here are four simple stages you can use to create an illustrated cartoon character.

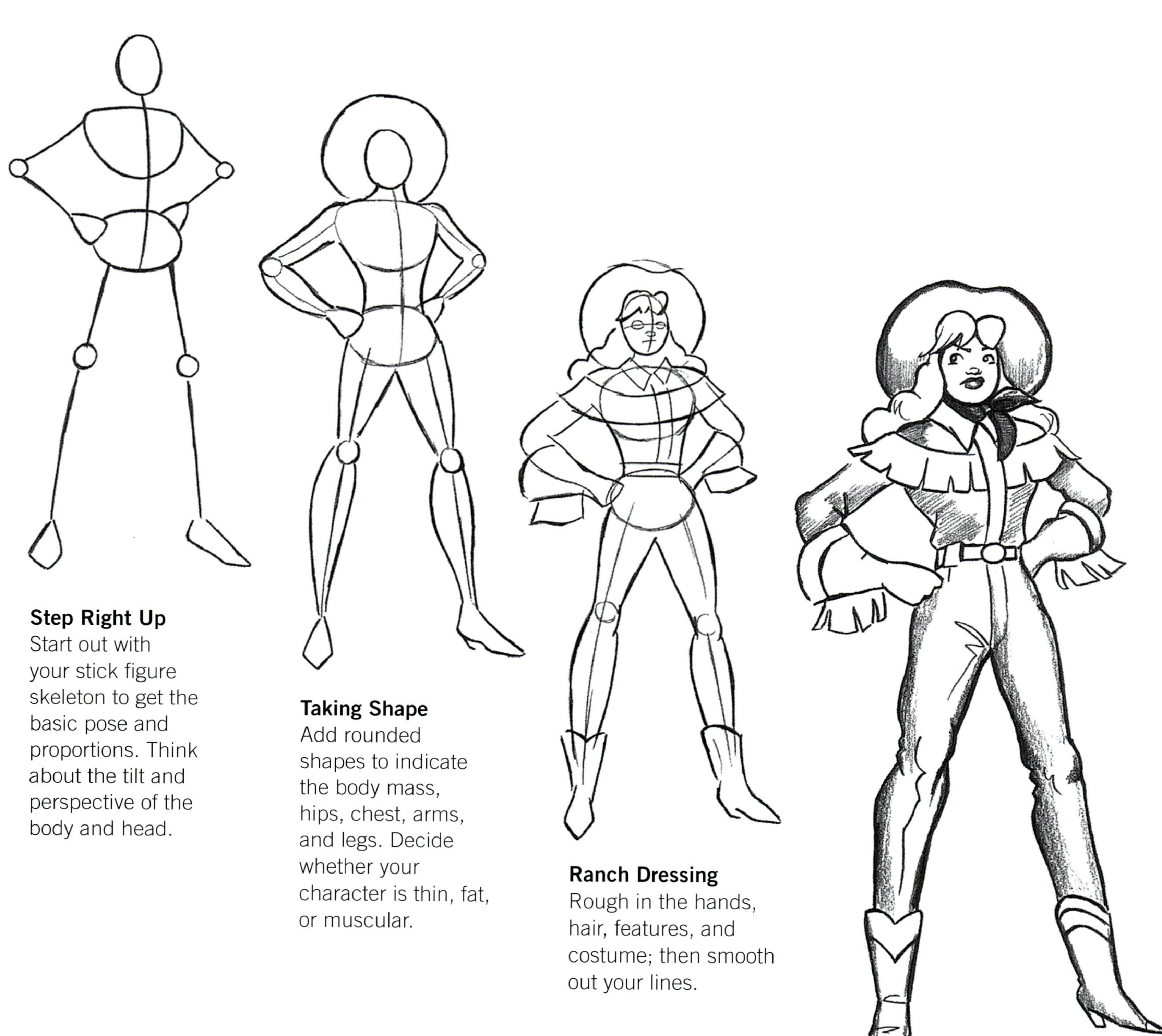

Step Right Up
Start out with your stick figure skeleton to get the basic pose and proportions. Think about the tilt and perspective of the body and head.

Taking Shape
Add rounded shapes to indicate the body mass, hips, chest, arms, and legs. Decide whether your character is thin, fat, or muscular.

Ranch Dressing
Rough in the hands, hair, features, and costume; then smooth out your lines.

Girl Howdy!
Now complete the final drawing, adding as much detail as you want. You've determined all the basics. Now on to the finished drawing. Have as much fun with detail as you want now.

Play Against Type

Superheroes are usually tall and heroic, but who's to say you can't create a hero who is short and slight? If so, pointed ears, a skintight space suit, and a flashy mask may be *de rigueur*. But what if your ideal hero turns out to be a mild-mannered cartoonist whose markers are really magic?

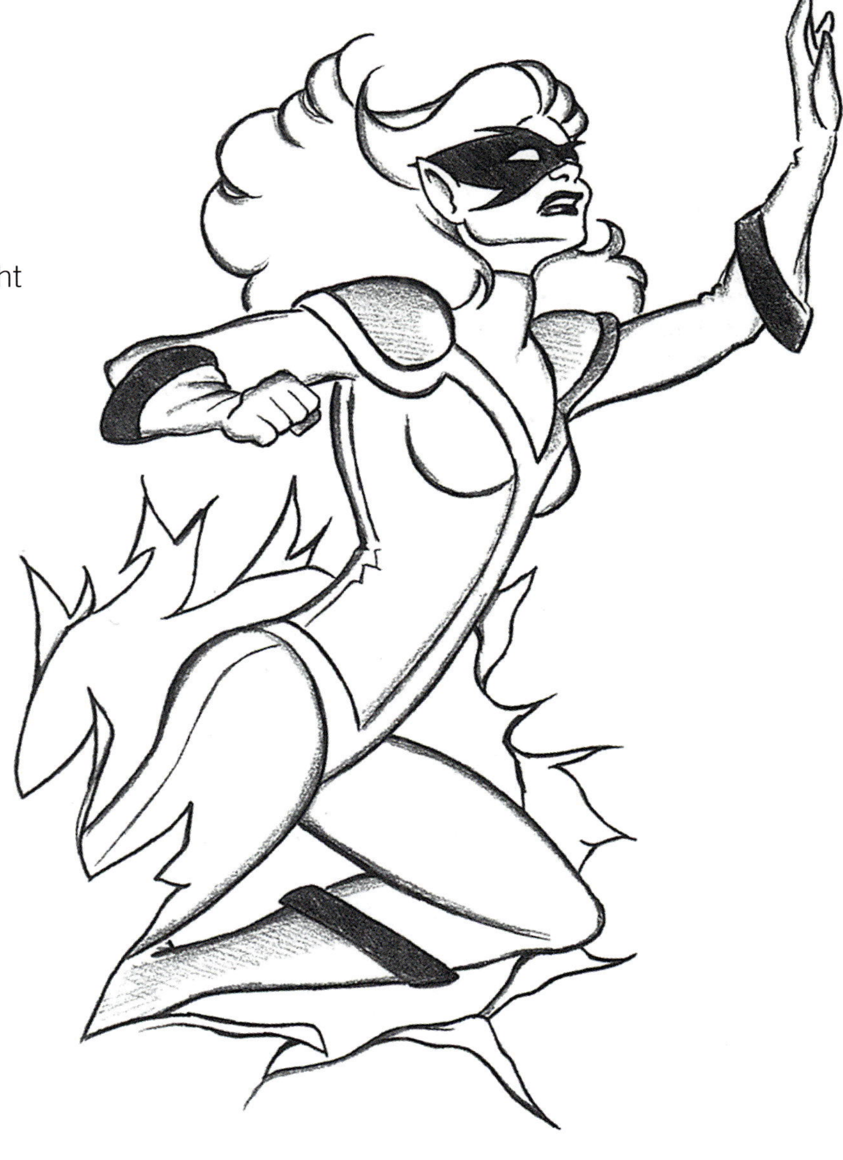

Handy Tips

Hands can be a challenge. For realistic 'toons, you'll need to show all ten fingers, so practice now. (Try drawing the hands below.) Steel fists, feeble fingers, plump palms, gnarled knuckles—each hand here has a unique personality depending on which aspects are emphasized.

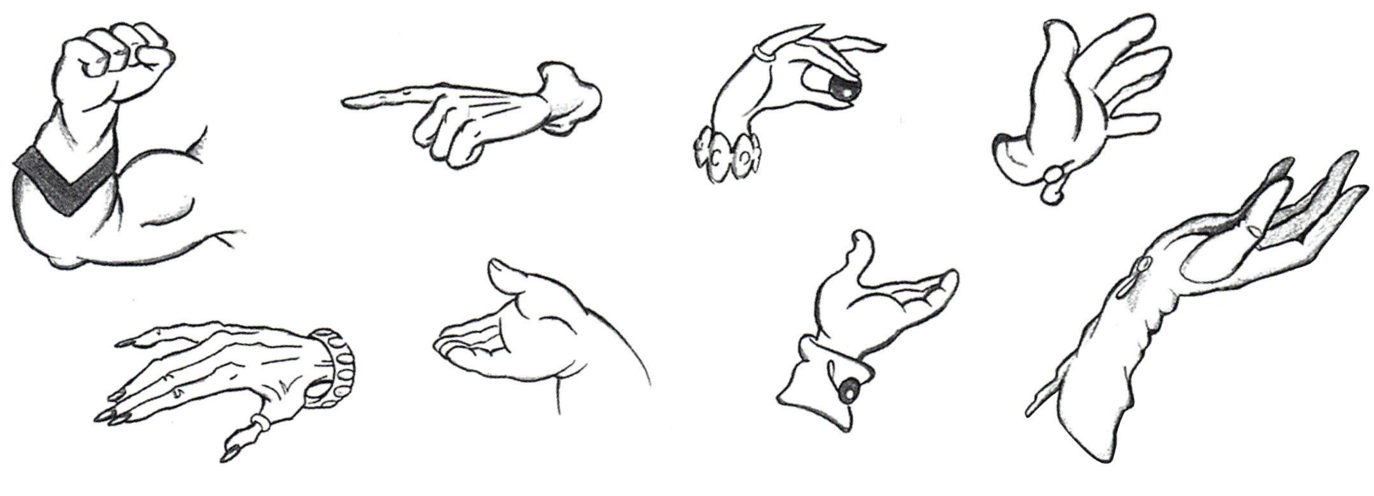

REALISTIC ROVER

Animals in illustrated cartoons must be rendered in a style consistent with their human counterparts, and they must be able to convey emotions. The goal is to create the impression of muscles, bone, feathers, and fur realistic enough to be believable, yet streamlined into cartoon shorthand. Facial features need to be humanized so they can then be exaggerated for effect.

START WITH A PHOTO

Photographic references can be helpful. Start with a realistic representation, and then simplify the animal, emphasizing its actions and expressions. Then let your creative juices loose: the photo should be a guide and inspiration, not a straightjacket.

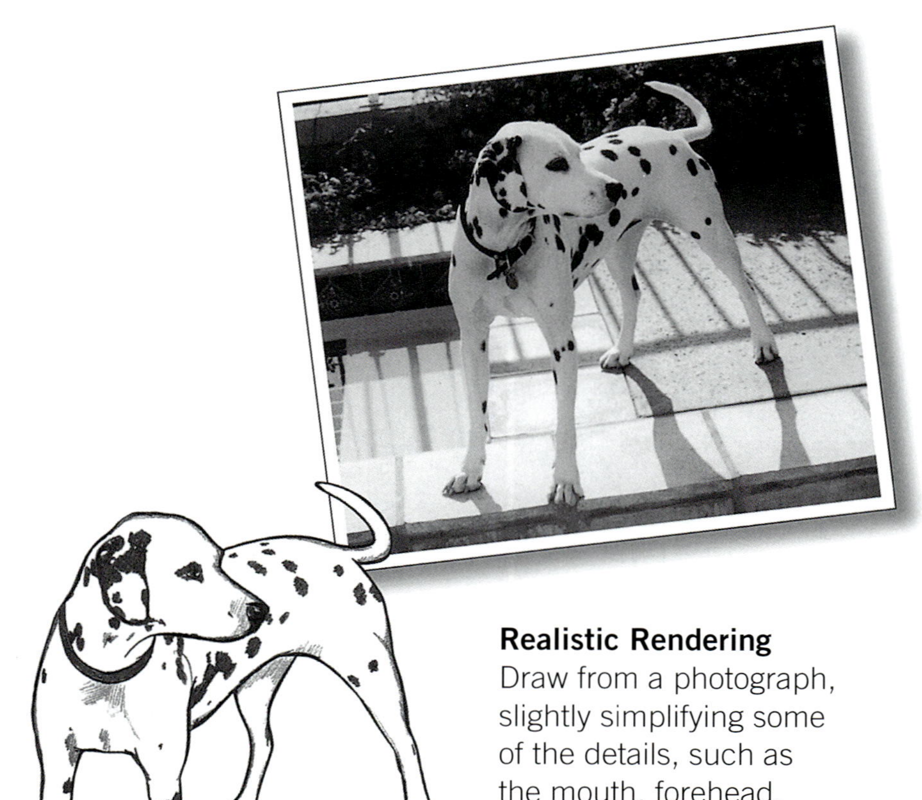

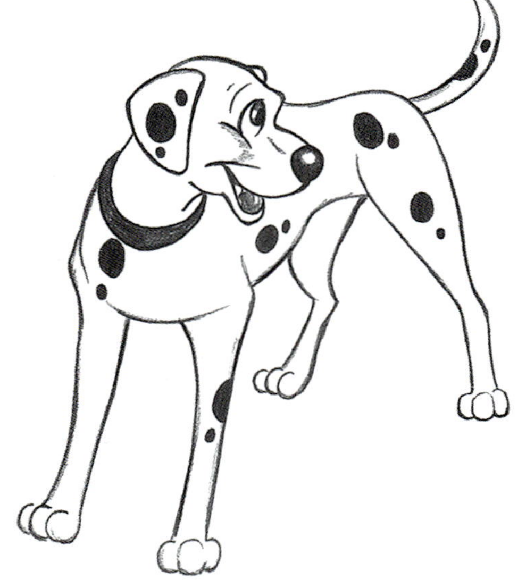

Realistic Rendering
Draw from a photograph, slightly simplifying some of the details, such as the mouth, forehead, and collar. However streamlined, this drawing is still solidly realistic.

Seeing Spots
Here is a "realistic" cartoon. The structure of the body and the pattern of the fur have been stylized, and, in typical cartoon fashion, her face and feet have been enlarged.

Going to Town
Alter the position and shape of the ear, enlarge the nose, bug out the eyes, and rubberize the limbs. Although recognizable as a Dalmatian, this dog has become a full-fledged zany.

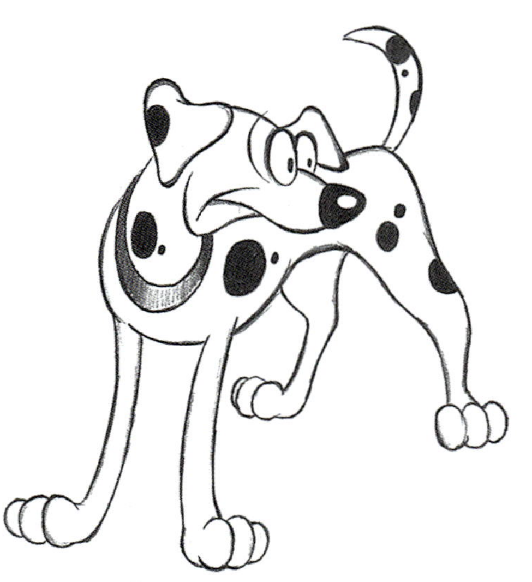

Tall Story
As with the Dalmatian, the eyes and ears of this wistful giraffe are larger, and his facial expression is far more human than you'd see on the real McCoy. His hooves have also been enlarged, and the design of his coat simplified.

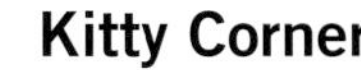

Kitty Corner
The tabby above was drawn in a simplified but fairly straightforward way. She's just an ordinary cat. The fat cat at right is a tad cartoonier, with his cranky nature reflected in an angry smirk. The slinky, seated cat below has been slenderized and elongated—but her demeanor is still pure feline.

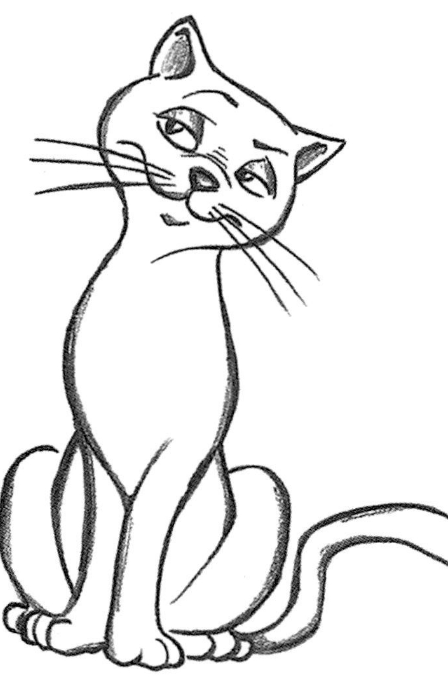

Wild Things
Jungle cats, such as this lioness, look a lot like their domesticated cousins, but they are more muscular and—with their powerful heads and large jaws—far more imposing. Follow the same procedure with these big cats: simplify the shapes and emphasize and enlarge the facial features.

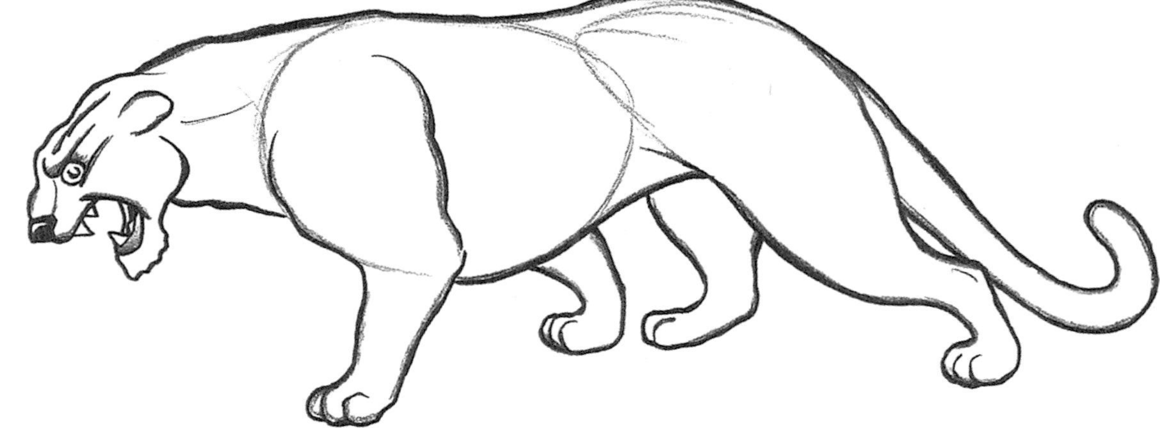

DRESS 'EM UP

As a cartoonist, you are not only the casting director and author of your cartoons, but the costume designer as well. Clothes make the man, as the saying goes, and you can get a lot of mileage out of the duds you choose for your "brainchildren."

ADD SOME DEFINITION

Costume is very important in defining a character. For instance, pin a star on a hound and he's instantly perceived as a law dog. Or draw a circle around the same hound's head to serve as a space helmet! Play up aspects of dress that make it clear what kind of character this is at a glance.

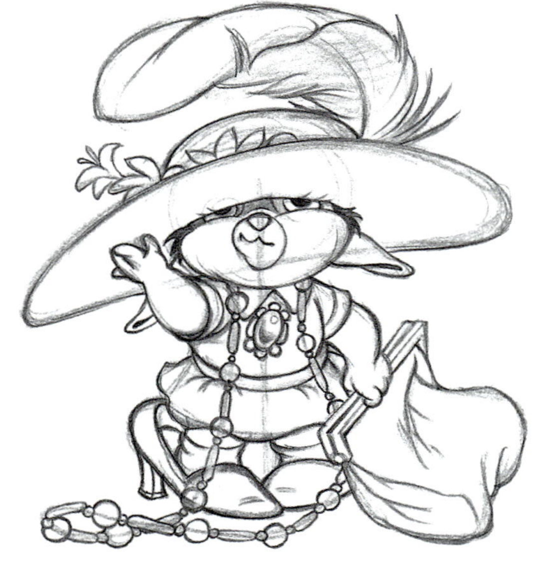

Playing Dress-Up
The oversized shoes, hat, and handbag tell the viewer that this little bunny is dressed in Mama's clothes.

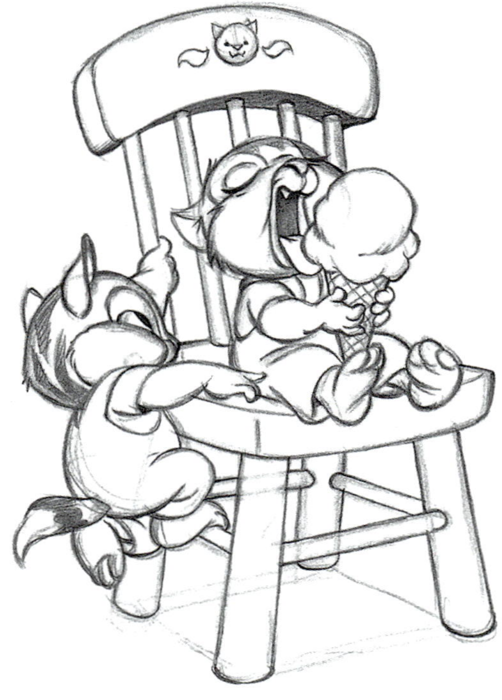

Kids Will Be Kids
Using big props on little kids is a surefire way to elicit the "Aww, isn't that cute" response.

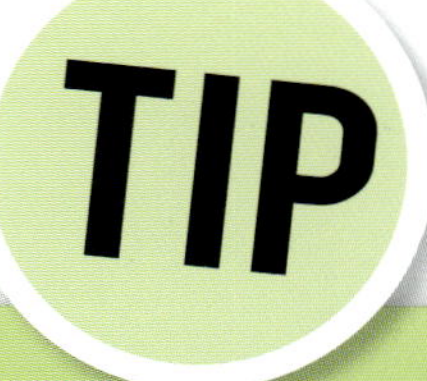

TIP

Because you may have to draw the same character over and over, you need to keep the wardrobe fairly simple. Pockets, zippers, and buttons may be necessary in real life, but not in a cartoon.

Quite a Crew
These characters started out as round-headed figures with pear-shaped bodies. Their clothing design and details, such as teeth and nails, came later.

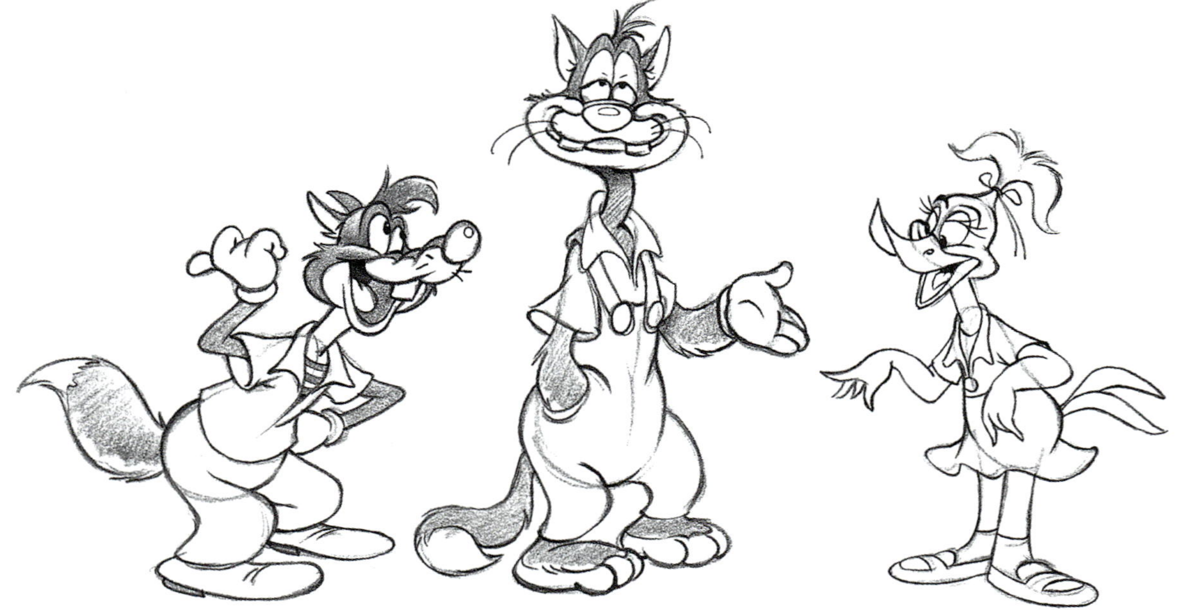

THE CLOTHES MAKE THE CARTOON

Your audience should understand your character's personality without reading a word. A scientist's lab coat, a movie star's mink stole, a rebel's leather jacket, or a spy's trench coat each help identify your players and tell your story.

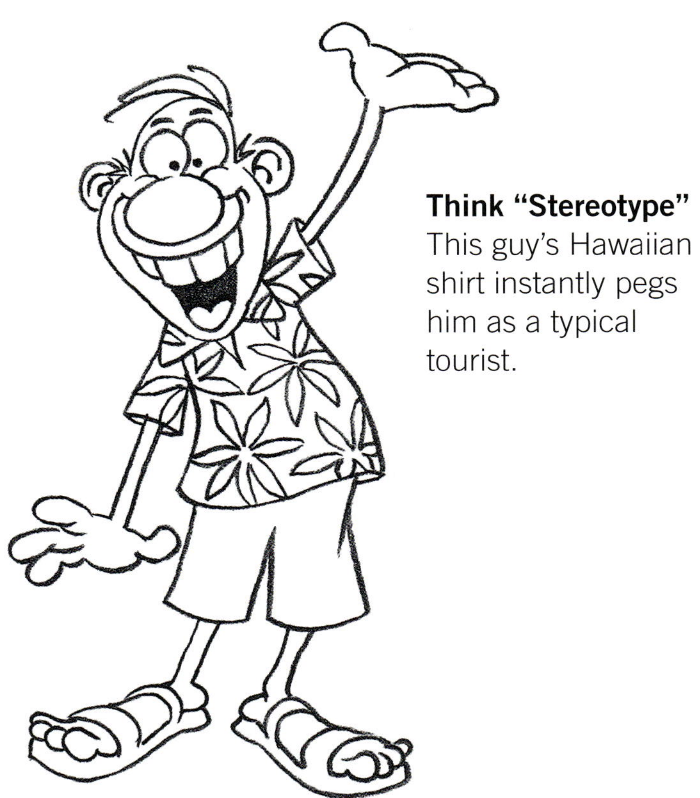

Think "Stereotype"
This guy's Hawaiian shirt instantly pegs him as a typical tourist.

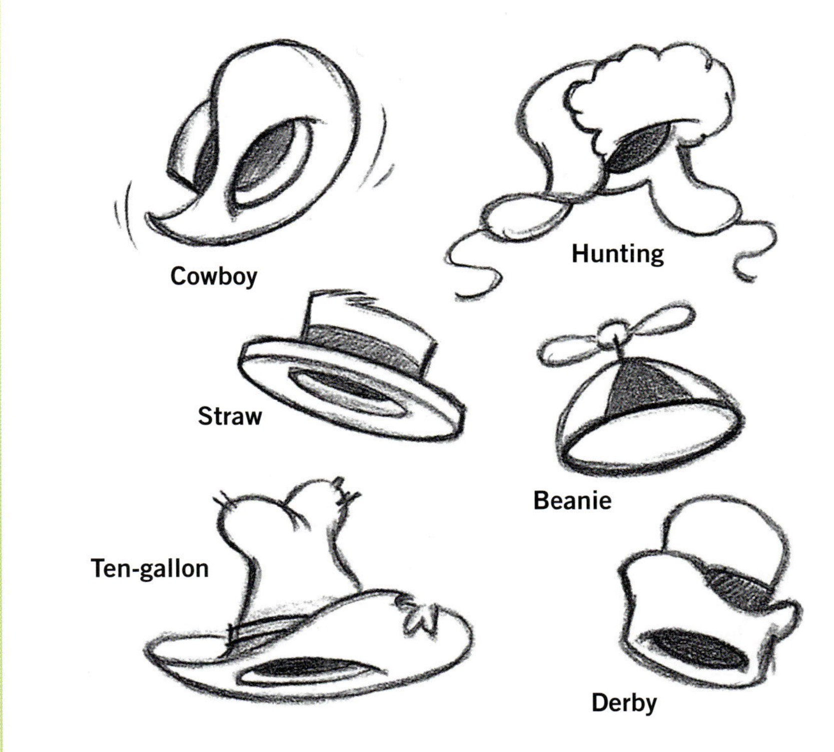

Put a Lid on It

A football helmet, baseball cap, or chef's hat will identify your character's occupation, but a playful propeller beanie, a weather-beaten ten-gallon hat, or a fur-lined cap will also give you distinct clues to a cartoon's personality.

WARDROBE!

A change of apparel can totally alter your perception of a character. Here, our chameleon has been given four distinct changes of costume, makeup, and coiffure, radically altering her personality.

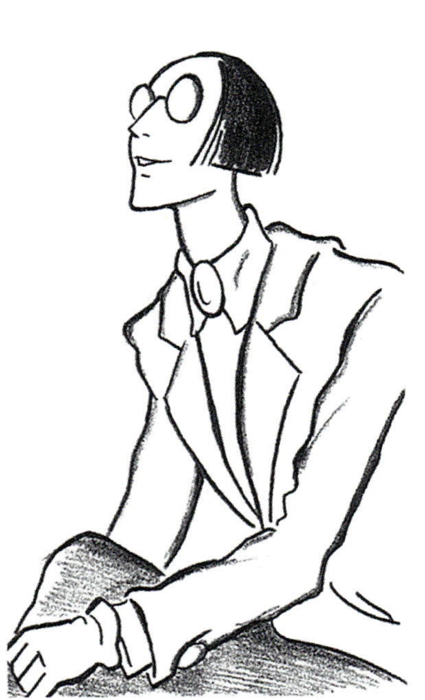

In Business Inspiring mogul Jane wears a suit and bob cut with class.

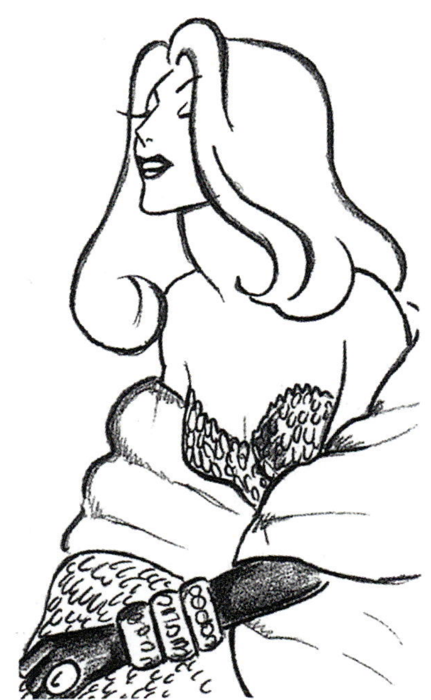

In Movies Peek-a-boo hair and some white mink give starlet Jane glamour.

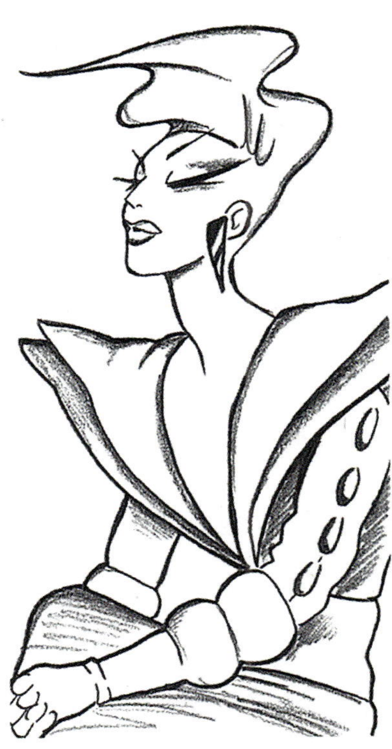

In Outer Space A space-age suit and gravity-defying hair make Jane ready for blast-off.

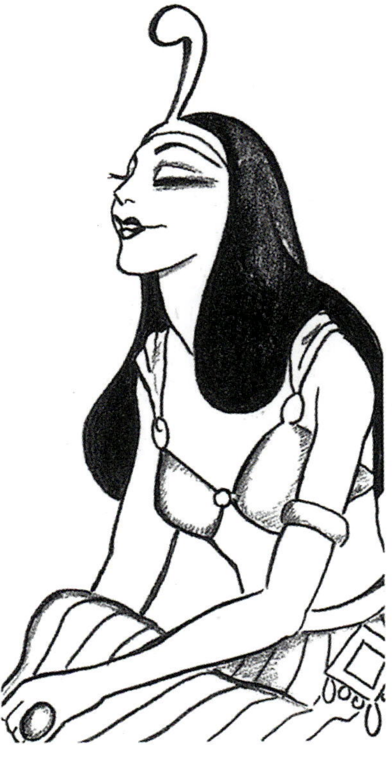

In "De Nile" A serpentine headdress and eyeliner turn Jane into Cleopatra.

TALKING TOASTERS & TREES

An animated cartoon may feature props, such as an old, sputtering jalopy, an obnoxious alarm clock, and a whistling teakettle brimming with personality. The props in your cartoons can also become players in the plot. An object may display a face, a voice, and the ability to move, truly becoming a character in the story—and, occasionally, the hero.

HOUSEHOLD HINTS

Telephones, mustard jars, radios, dishwashers, and other household objects can be drawn with lots of bounce and style. As with human characters—exaggerate and simplify! Too much detail bores the viewer and makes the picture needlessly complicated. You may choose to forget about adding limbs and hands when giving personality to inanimate objects. You can play off of what's there already, allowing table legs to dance or the cord of an appliance to become as agile as a monkey's tail.

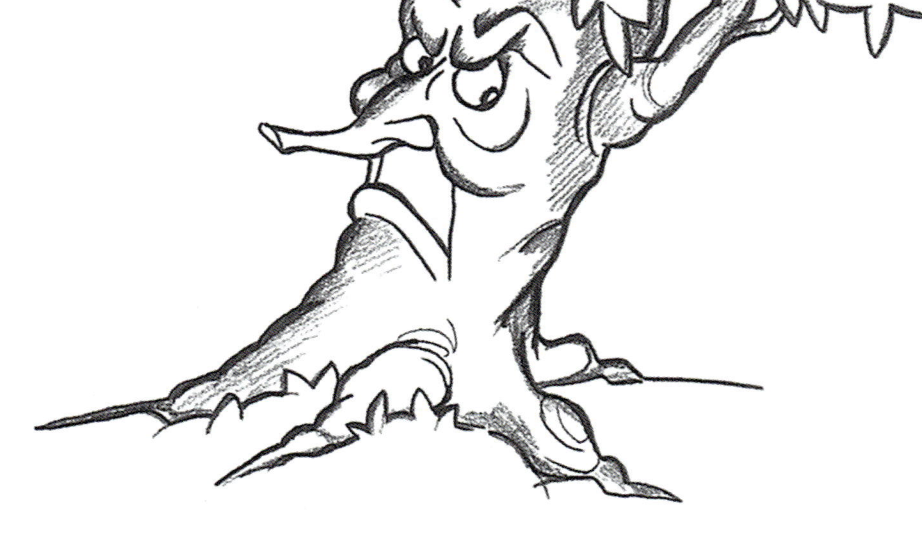

Branch Out

This sour apple tree's bark is worse than its bite. Tree branches often look like noses, arms, and fingers. The knotholes and lumps in tree bark can suggest cheeks, eyes, and mouths. Why not see what kind of personality you can craft for a weeping willow or a quaking aspen?

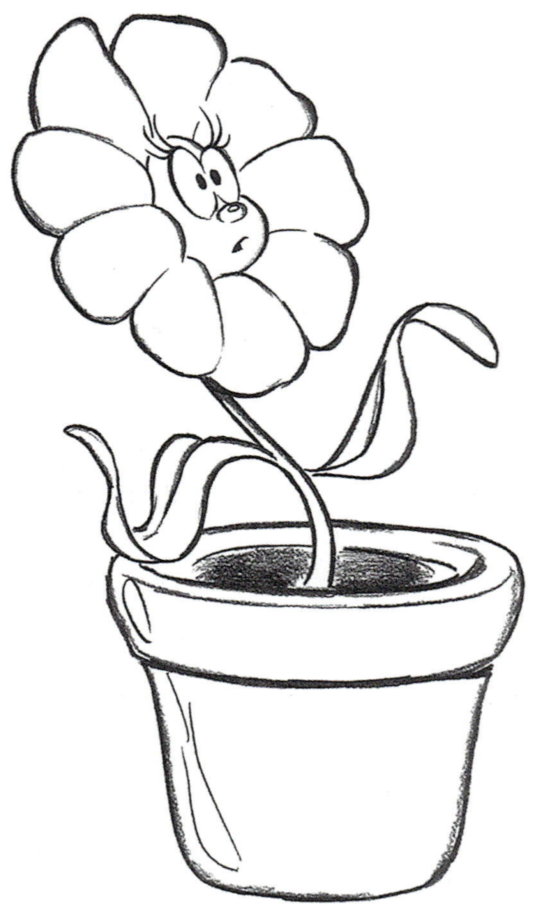

Wallflower

The slender stem and delicate leaves provide Flora with a bendable torso and expressive arms, and the flower pot echoes a skirt. She is fully humanized, even though the only real fantasy element added is her face.

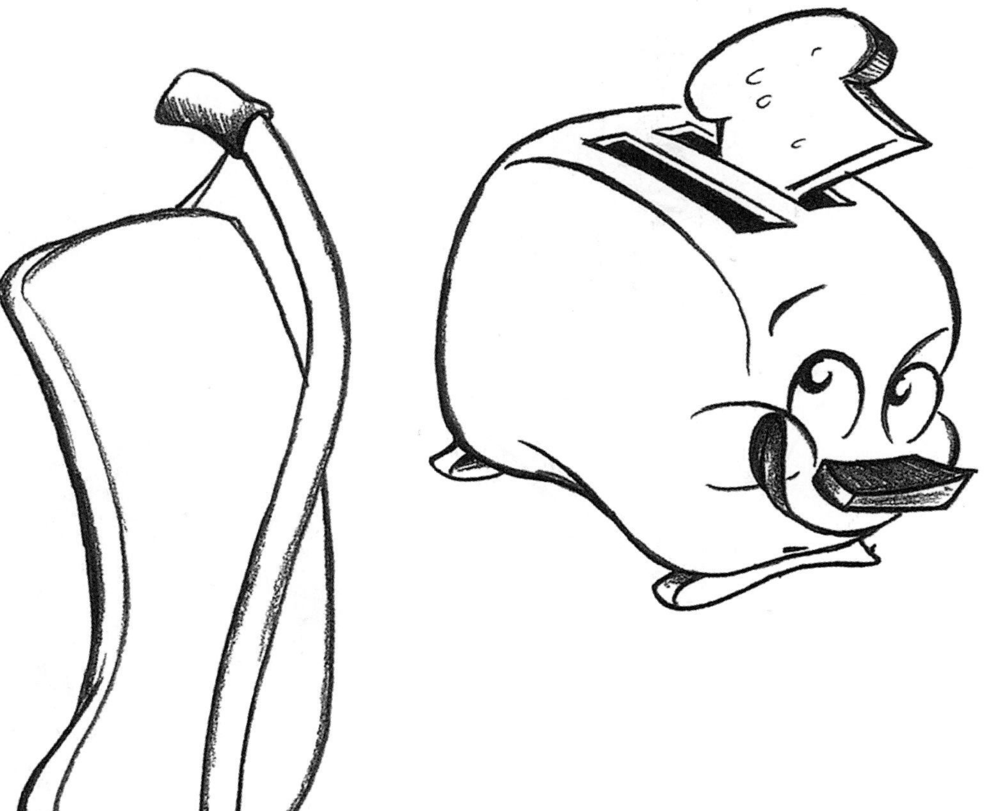

Appliances with Attitude

With a wave of your magic pencil, you can bring any inanimate object to life. Frequently, a face is all that's needed to wake up a vacuum cleaner or add a little "pop!" to a personable toaster.

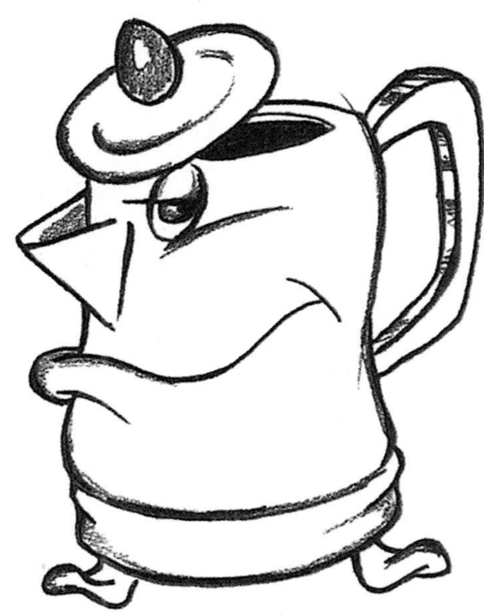

Pick a Personality

French-roasted coffee has gone to this percolator's head, and he now wears his lid as a snappy beret. It's fun to play off the personalities that different objects suggest. For example, does the sugar bowl have a sweet tooth? Or does the pepper mill make the salt shaker sneeze?

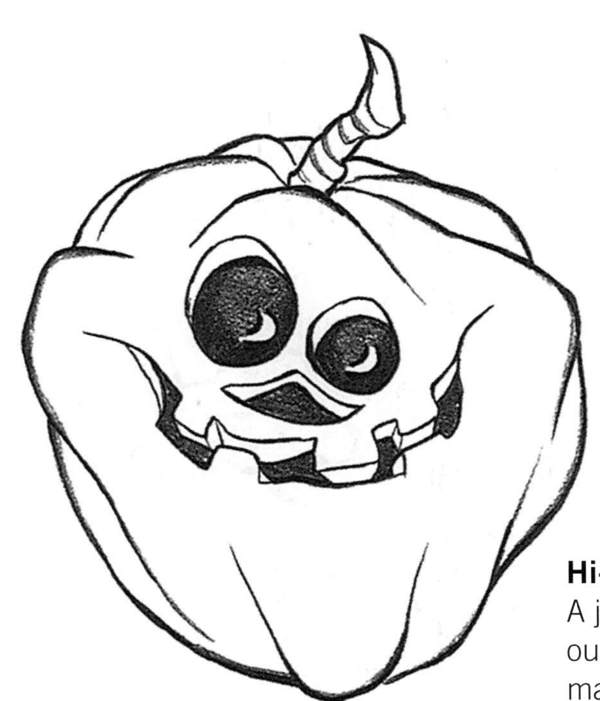

Hi-Jack

A jack-o-lantern is sort of an outlandish subject to start with, making it great fun to cartoon.

CAR-TOONS

A grumbling old pickup truck? A jaunty jalopy? A sultry sports car?
What personalities do the vehicles you see every day suggest to you?

TIP

The hard metal skin of an auto becomes soft and supple in a cartoon. Think of the vehicles you draw as being made out of very soft, pliable rubber rather than of steel.

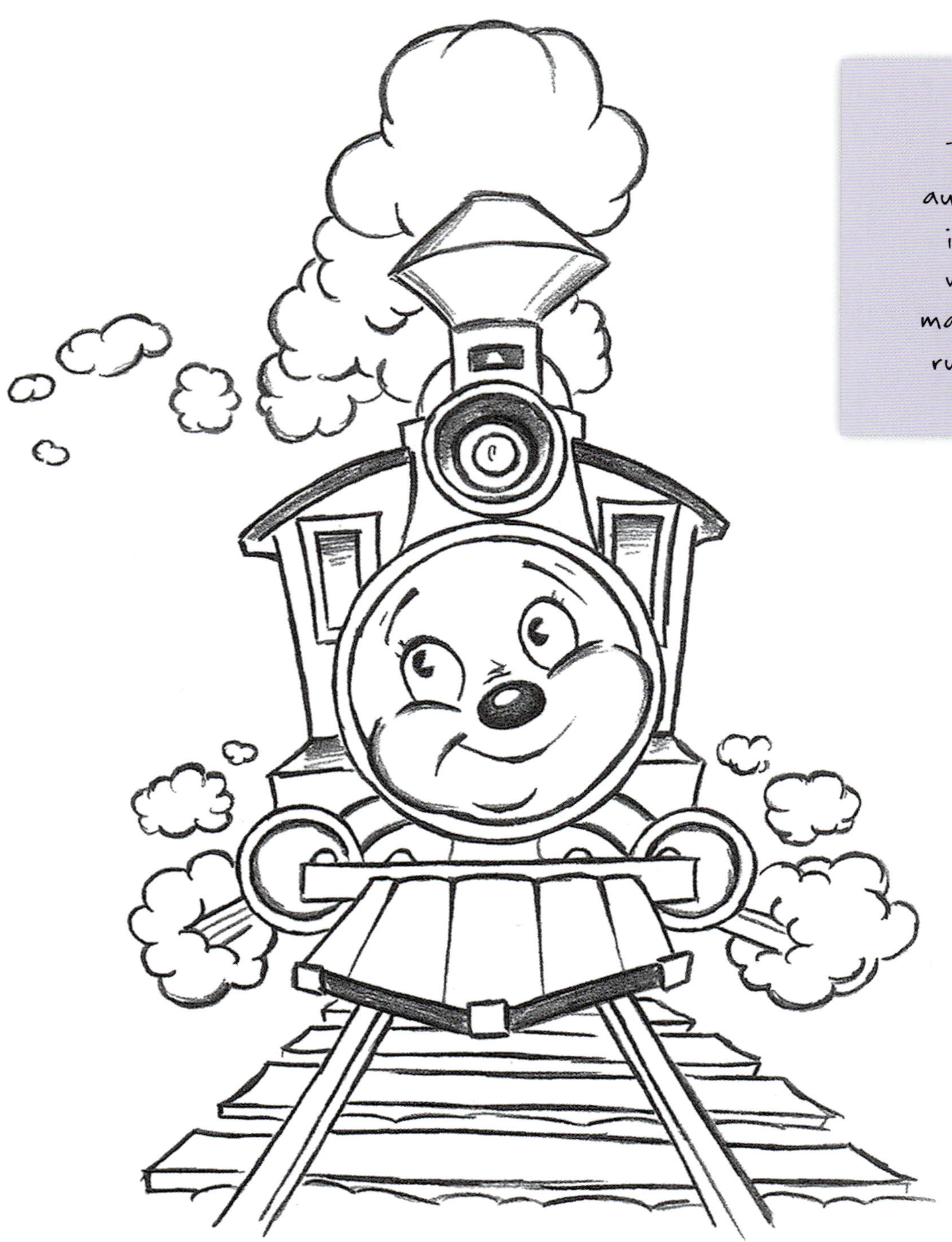

Trains
Puffs of smoke get smaller as they fade into the distance, making this happy little engine appear to chug toward you.

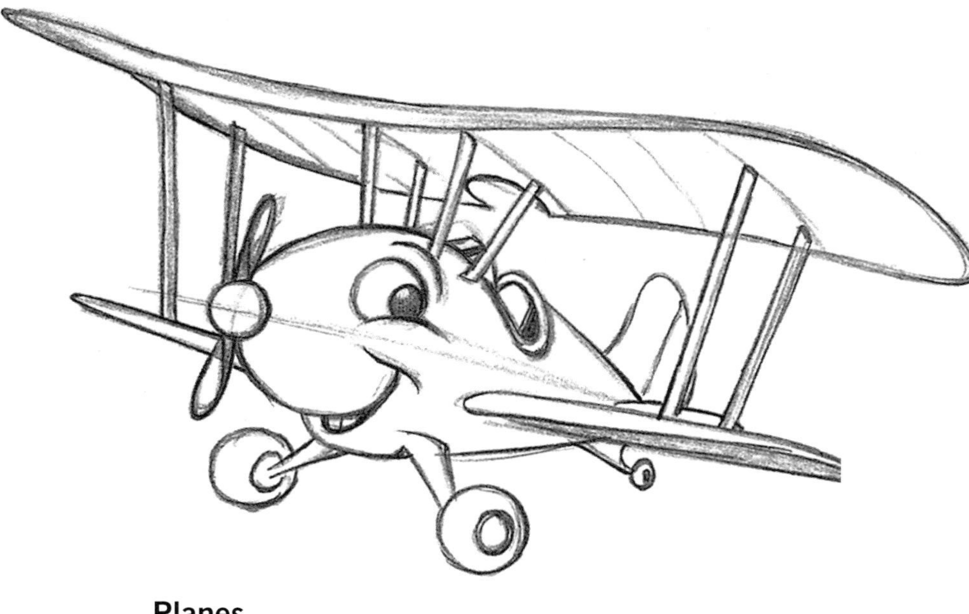

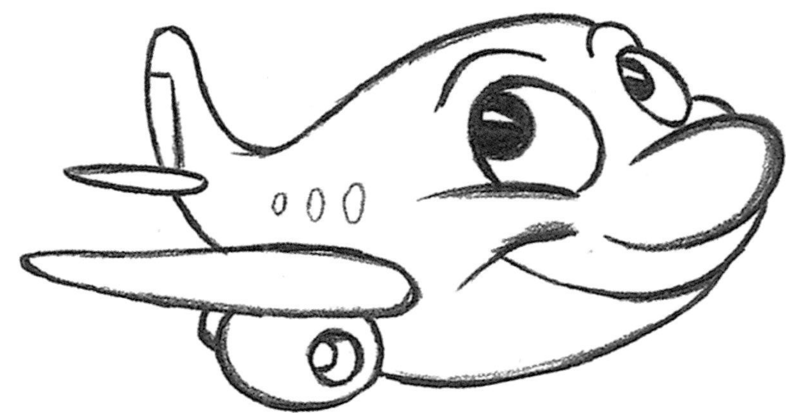

Planes

Vintage sports cars, small planes, and tugboats are kind of round and puffy in the first place—perfect for cute and cuddly cartoon characters. Emphasize these aspects with softly curving lines. The front windows of this little jet easily translate into a pair of eyes. The biplane's propellers make a natural nose, and its wings and wheels suggest arms and legs.

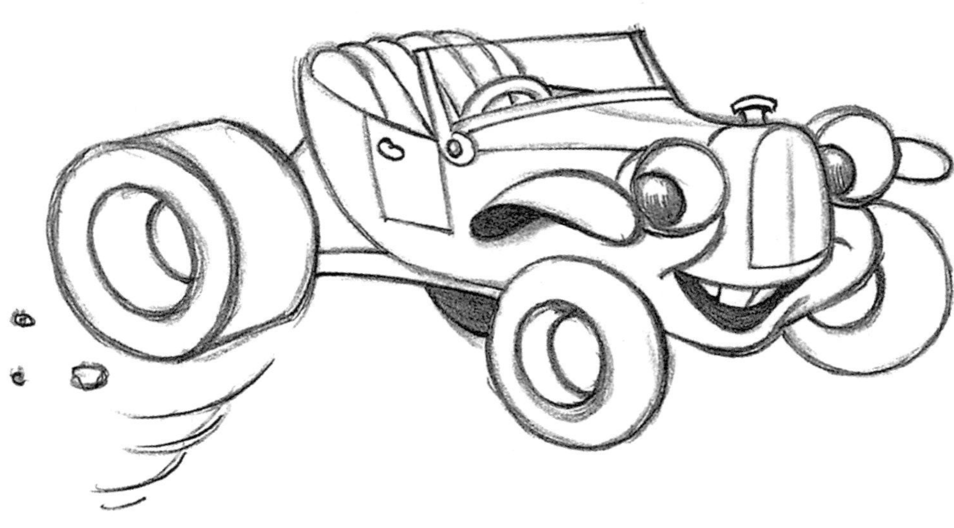

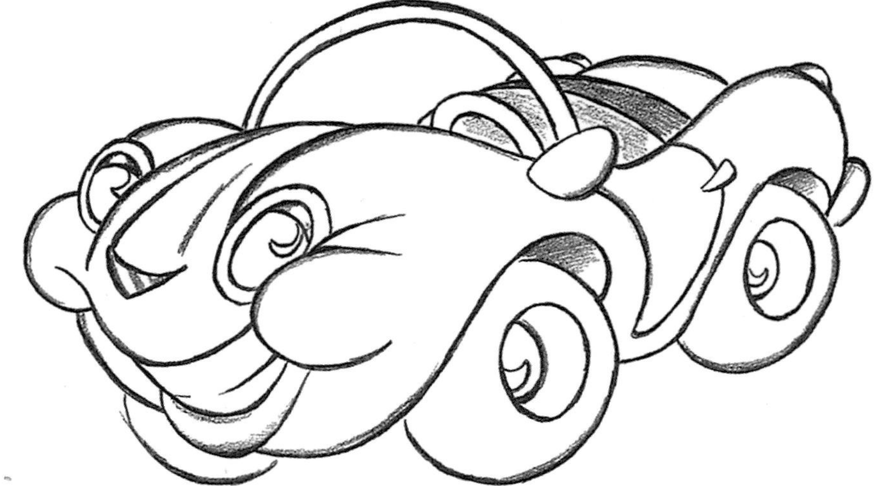

And Automobiles

A car is made up of hundreds of parts, but you don't need to doodle all of them. Here only the elements that define the identity and amplify the personality of this spunky hot rod and silky sports car are used. Edit out as many extra details as possible. Remember, simplify, simplify, simplify!

LOCATION

When you draw cartoons, you will also design props to heighten the mood and strengthen the story line of his cartoon. The choice of which props to use depends on whether it's a jungle saga or a big-city crime drama, whether it takes place in the future or the Stone Age, and whether or not it's intended to amuse, thrill, or chill.

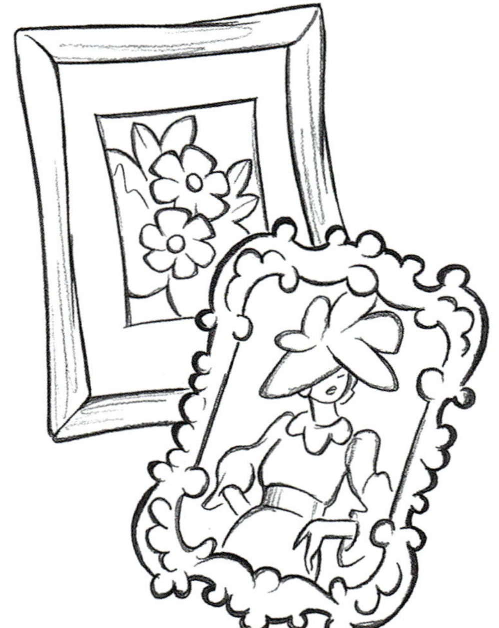

Picture This

Just a few details in the background are often enough to pin down a locale. An oriental rug on the floor or a picture on the wall can flesh out an interior. Does your scene require a homey still life or something in a gilded frame?

Housing Project

Even houses can be designed to have a whimsical cartoon personality. Softening the lines of the roof and walls accentuate the warmth of this country cottage.

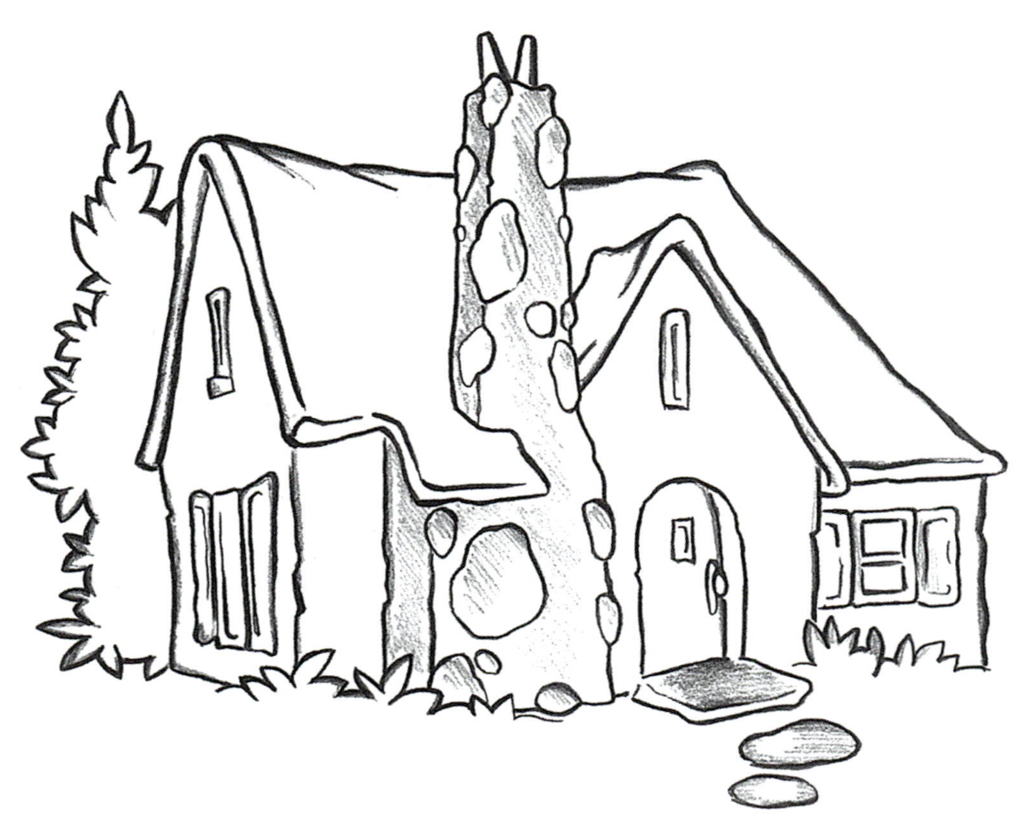

In the Doghouse

A water bowl and bone help this doghouse feel like a castle. The individual boards of the roof suggest the architect was a 10-year-old.

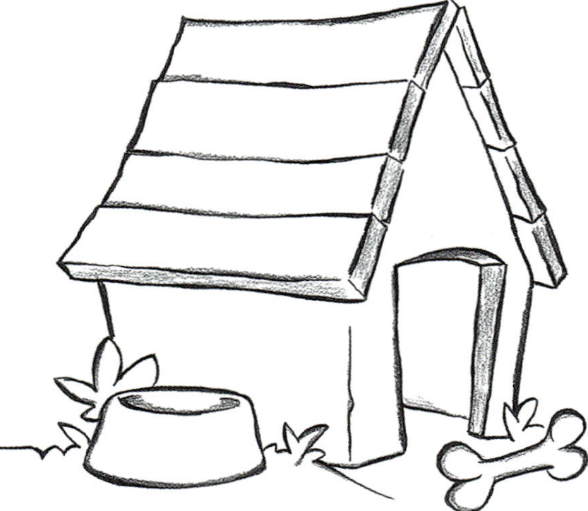

Accessorize

Subtle or not-so-subtle distortion adds personality to mundane objects. The fat forms of this dripping faucet accentuate its humor. This alarm clock stretches and squashes as it clangs away.

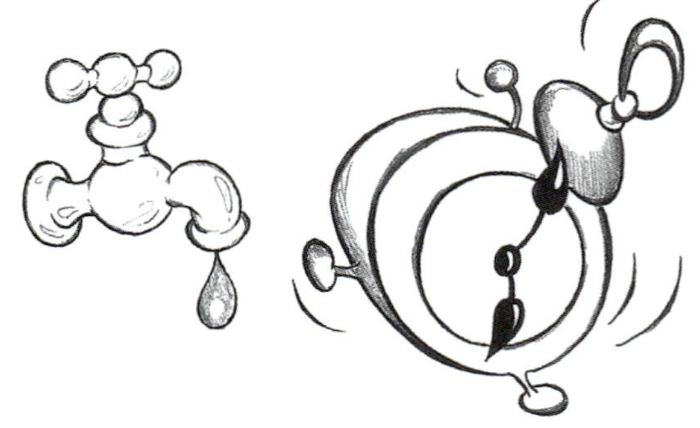

CREATING A CARTOON STORY

When deciding on props and backgrounds, have a clear idea of where the action is taking place and the type of props that should logically appear. Then select only the props that are essential. Don't confuse the viewer with clutter.

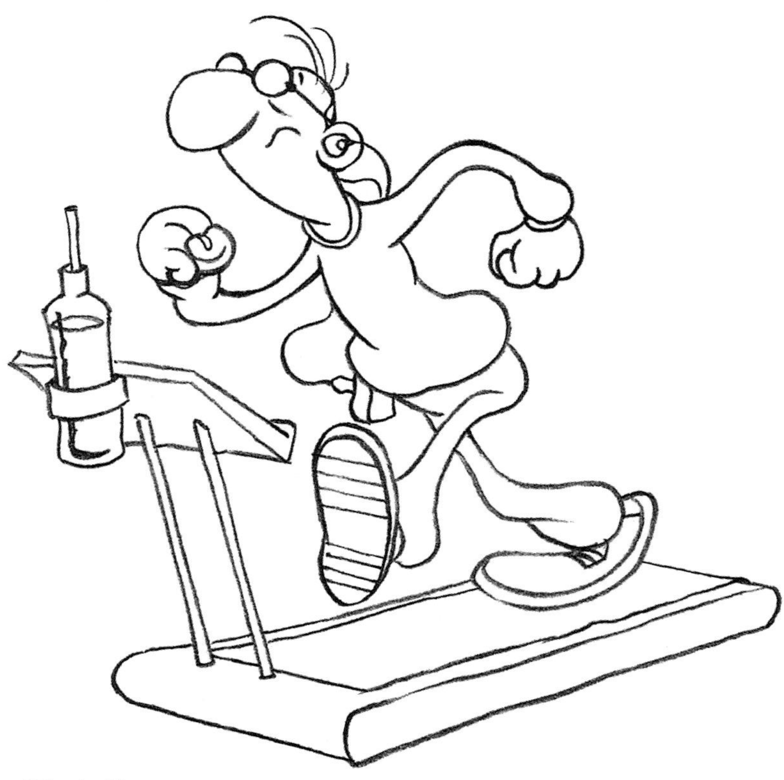

Work It
Let's say your main man needs some exercise. Give him some decent sweats and running shoes, maybe a bottle of water, and some headphones. With a few details you've suggested an environment. Feel the burn!

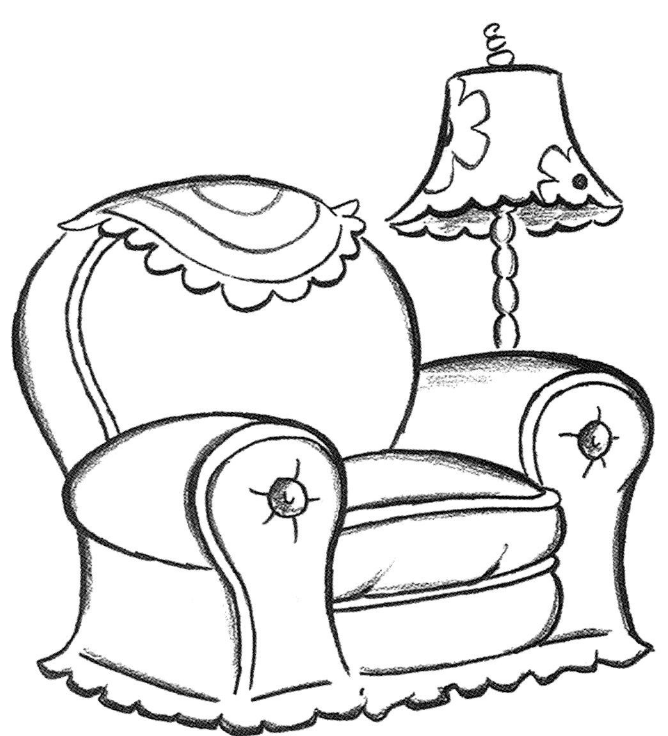

Let's Relax
Okay, the workout's over, and your cartoon hero could use a comfortable place to take a load off. The chair and lamp above are neat and respectable. But perhaps the style is a little more suited to Grandma.

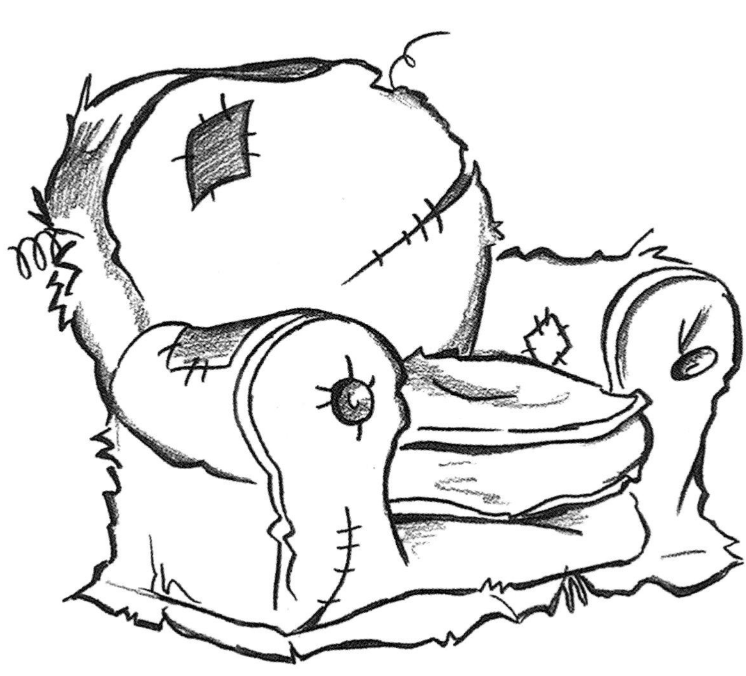

Pretty Shabby
With a few adjustments, the whole mood is altered drastically. Oops—too much! Now the style is "early haunted house."

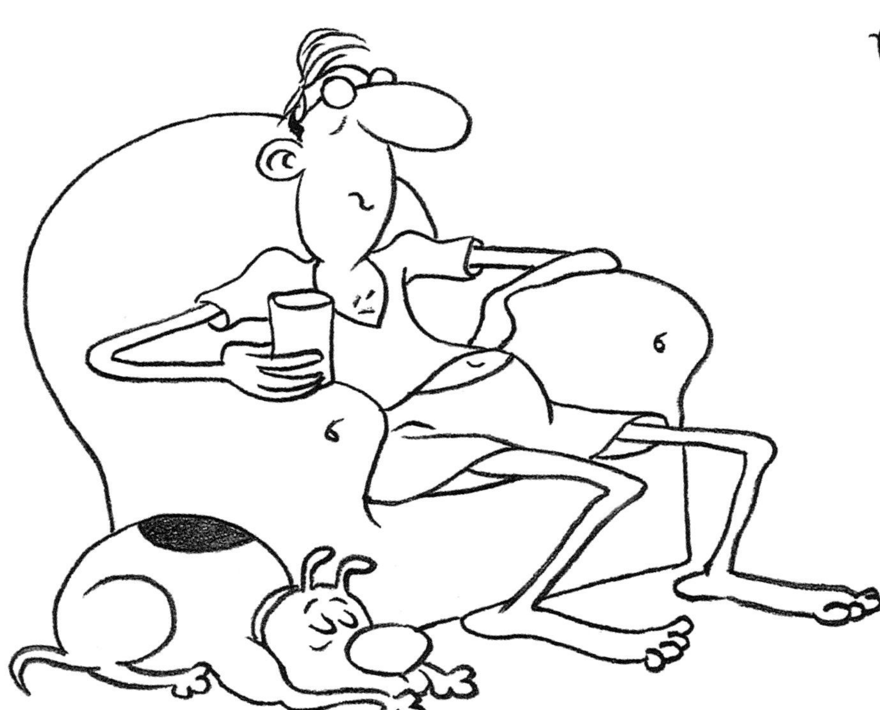

Setting the Stage
This guy just needs the simple things in life. A comfy chair, a cold drink, and a best pal. Ahhh ... perfecto!

CREATING A MODEL SHEET

When you have a character you really like and plan to draw a lot, put together a model sheet like the one shown here. A model sheet is a group of drawings of a character in a variety of poses and expressions and from a bunch of different angles. This will help you (and your team of assistants) keep your character consistent from one drawing to the next.

MODEL CITIZEN

When developing a model sheet of your original character, try to include all of its different poses and expressions—walking and talking, twisting and turning, winking and blinking. Remember, you are the creator, so you get to make all the decisions. Have fun with it!

Theodore Bear Model Sheet

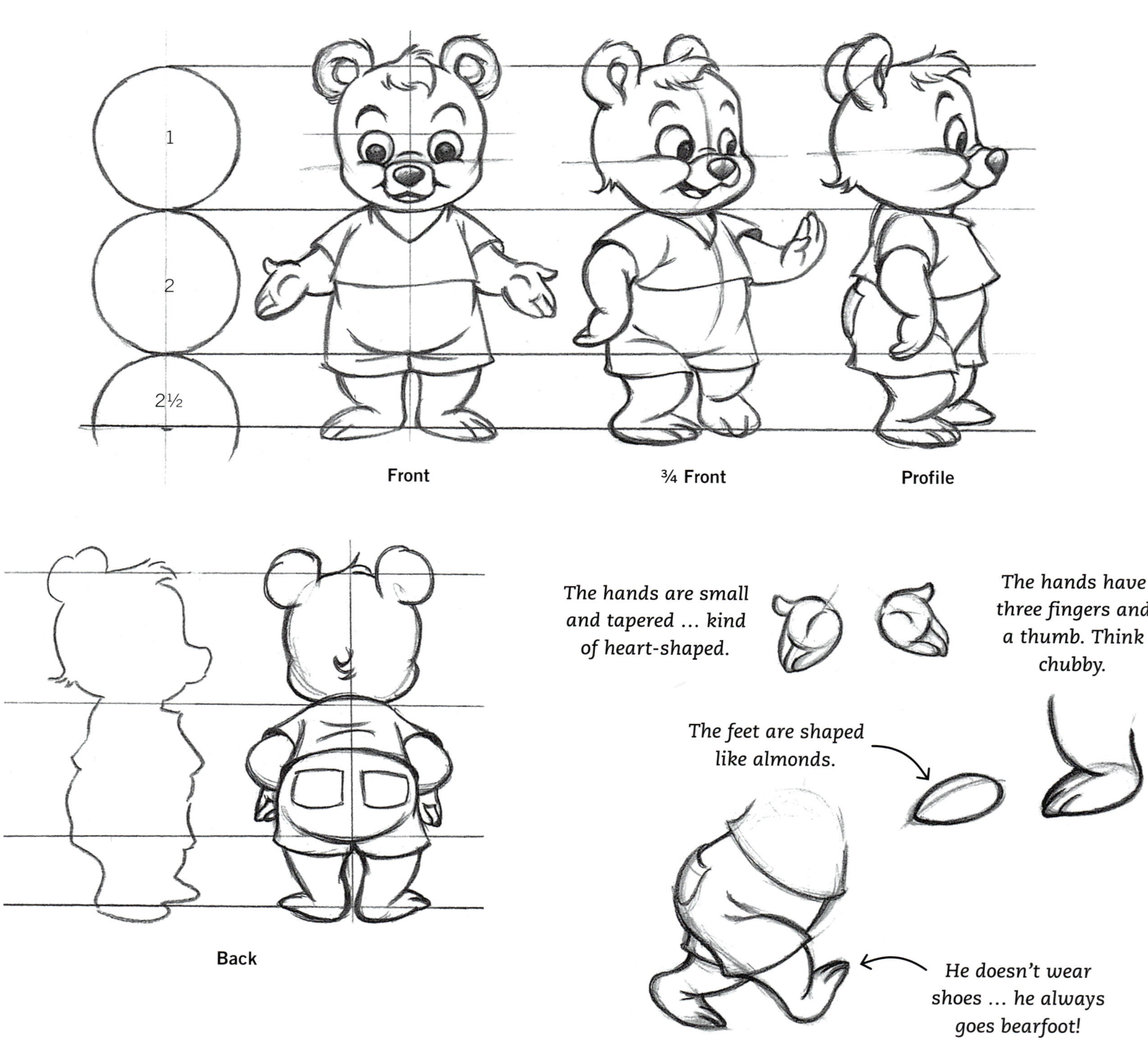

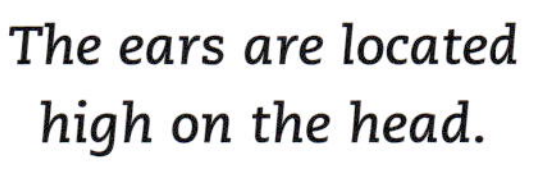

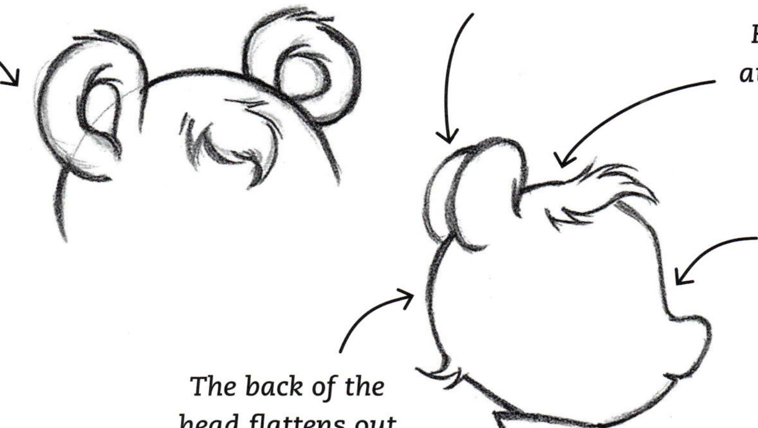

Expressions

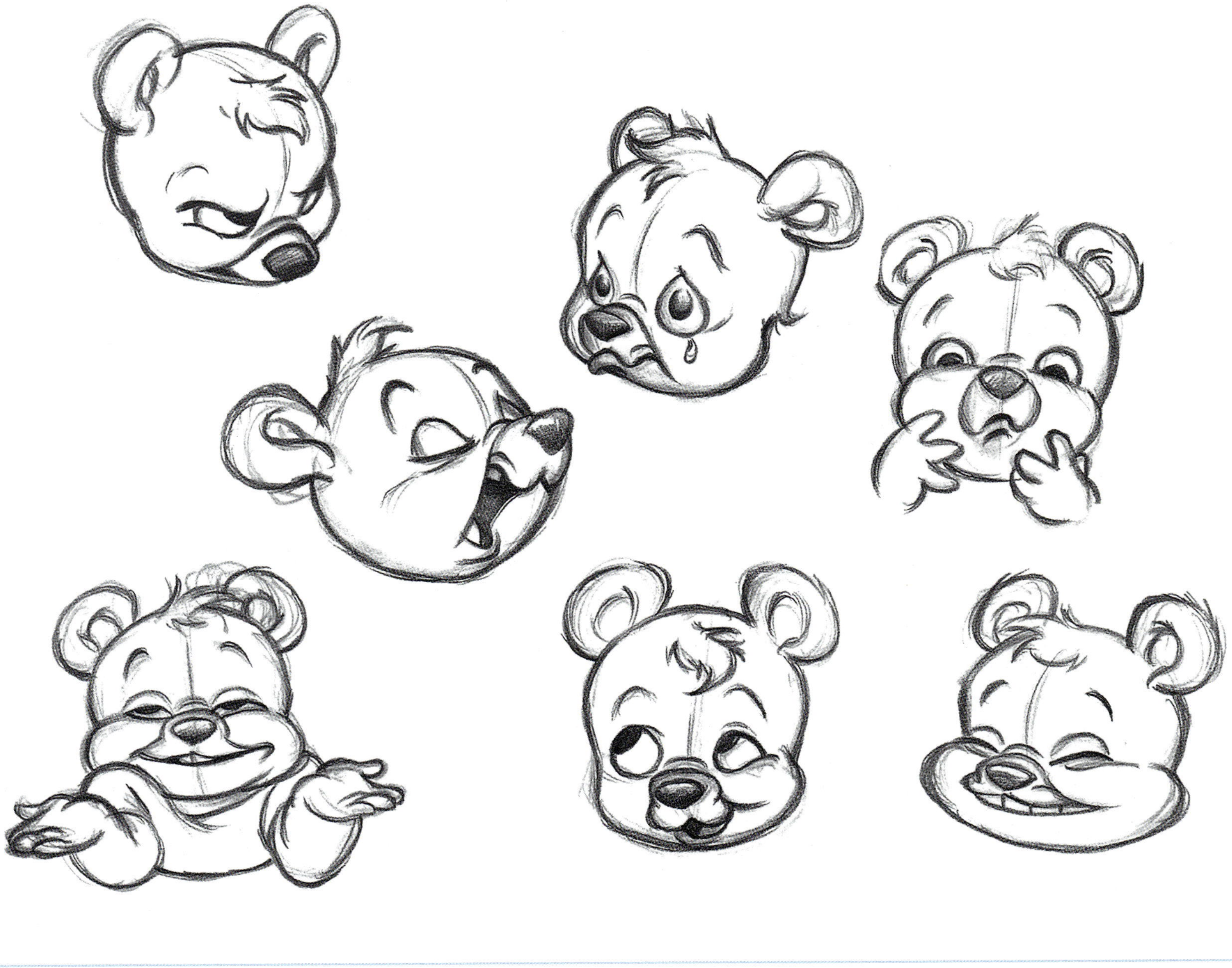

PERSONAL STYLE

As you continue to draw and create cartoon characters, you'll develop a style that's unique to you. The guidelines in this book can help you chart your own unique course. But remember, every rule can be broken!

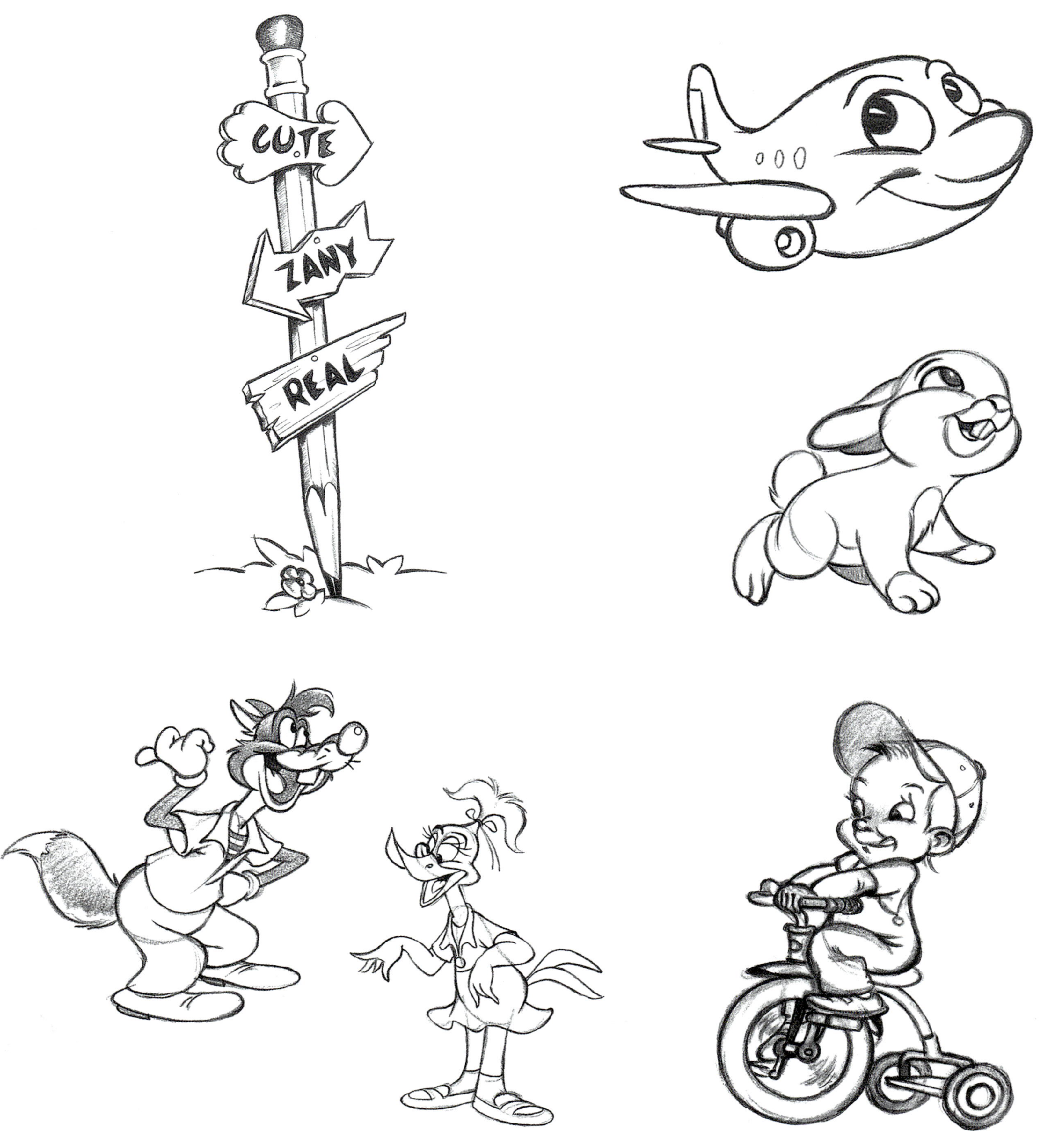